One World Library

Aldo Marcuzzi

THE WORLD OF CHEMISTRY

Research Luigina Sorrentino
Translated by Irene Anderson
Editor Richard Felton

Frederick Warne

First published in Great Britain by Frederick Warne (Publishers)
Ltd, London, 1980

© *Dotam BV (NL)*

© *1979 Malipiero spa Editore, Ozzano E., Italy*

English translation © *1980 by Frederick Warne (Publishers) Ltd,*
London

ISBN 0 7232 2331 9

Printed in Italy

Contents

Introduction

To most people chemistry is a subject that is difficult to understand, but it is really only a study of what things are made of. To gain an understanding of what chemistry means to us today we have to look at the world around us and at the everyday things that we take for granted such as food, plastics, clothes and medicines. All these things have been made by people discovering what things are made of and using that know-how to make new ones.

Chemistry is vital to the modern world, especially in industry and agriculture. Farmers, for example, use fertilizers developed by chemists to increase crops while modern industry depends on chemists to discover new substances and find out more about those already known.

But chemistry as we know it is a young science. Many of its roots lie in *alchemy*, an art that flourished until the Middle Ages. The followers of the art, alchemists as they were known, claimed to be able to change metals such as iron and lead into gold and silver. But by the Middle Ages people were starting to see through the tricks of the trade and alchemy fell into disrepute. Scientists started seriously to try to find out what things were made of and why they acted as they did. In this book we will give you an up-to-date view of the exciting advances made by chemists and how chemistry affects our modern world.

Below Chemistry helps agriculture by making the fertilizers which help crops like these fir trees grow faster and bigger. Fossil fuels like coal and anthracite are both important sources of chemicals.

1   What is chemistry?

From the earliest times man has been aware that the world is made of different things. The discovery of new materials and their use to us has given names ·to important periods of our history such as the Bronze and Iron Ages. We first of all learned to use chemicals that occurred naturally to make useful things. Flints were used for tools and weapons, crushed plants for dyes and medicines. But this was long before anyone thought of why these things could be used as they were.

The answer to that lies in their chemistry. And

Left A few elements like gold occur naturally in a pure state. This gold nugget was washed from an ore deposit by a stream. **Below** The chemical industry today means production on a huge scale such as this petrol refining plant which covers many square kilometres.

Medieval alchemist

15th-century distillation apparatus

modern chemistry is the study of the substances that have been found to be the basic building blocks of the world—the *elements*. These basic elements can combine together to form all sorts of new substances called *compounds*.

At the start, whatever could not be explained was put down to magic. From this grew the art of alchemy. It became the search for the 'philosophers' stone'—a magical substance that could turn ordinary metals like iron into a precious metal such as gold. Alchemy was an attempt by early thinkers and practical chemists to explain things that today we take for granted. Of course the search was unsuccessful because the 'philosophers' stone' did not exist. But the hundreds of years of experiments did not go entirely to waste when alchemy eventually led to the science of modern chemistry.

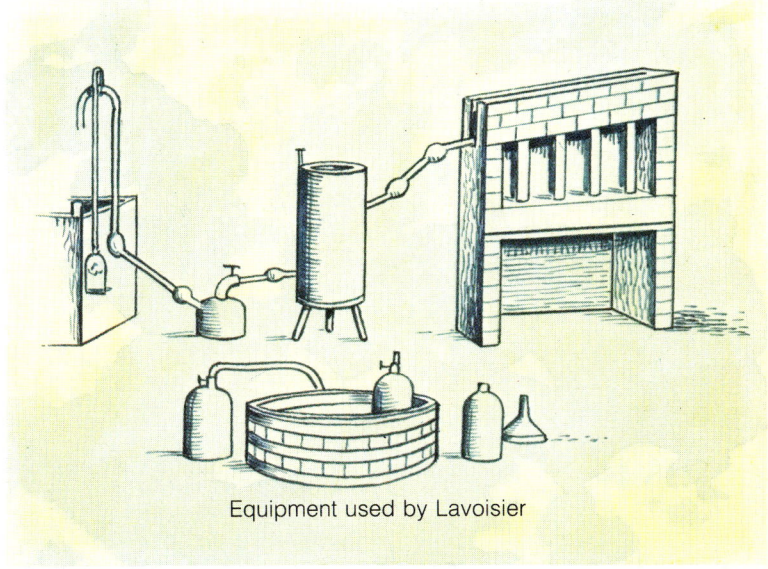
Equipment used by Lavoisier

Above This display of glass and ceramics is only available today because of discoveries made in the laboratory. **Left** A more familiar chemical reaction known to all of us is the rusting of iron by water. Rust is an oxide of iron.

The alchemists discovered the four natural elements—fire, air, earth and water—as well as some interesting facts about chemicals. Even so, the first major steps in the new science of chemistry had to wait until the eighteenth century. A French aristocrat called Lavoisier noticed that air appeared to be consumed when things burned. His theory that oxygen from the air combined with the burning substance was correct. The new substance formed is called an *oxide*.

Lavoisier's untimely death during the French Revolution did not stop other chemists from seizing on his ideas and following them up. Even so, another hundred years were to pass before there was enough evidence gathered together for a Russian chemist, Mendeleev, to advance a theory about the elements that stands to this day. Mendeleev devised a chart of the elements then known which he called the *Periodic Table* (see page 69). When he first set the chart out, not all the elements had been discovered. But the beauty of his system was that he was able to describe what the missing elements would look like and how they would react.

Scientists had thus been given a plan and they set out to fill the gaps. Mendeleev had grouped together the 'families' of elements which showed similarities into eight columns. Eventually chemists proved that there were 92 elements that occurred naturally. The complete table shows at a glance all the elements and their relationship to each other.

The elements are important to a chemist because they are his basic working tools. Thousands of people are today employed working on ways to combine elements together to make new substances—or compounds— which are useful. Elements cannot be broken down by chemical processes, so chemists are more concerned with bringing them together to make compounds. For example, sketching charcoal is made up of the element carbon. But it is this same element, carbon, that forms the basis for substances such as plastics and petrol.

The *atom* is the smallest part of any element that can take part in a chemical process. Many millions of them go to make up even the tiniest speck of charcoal. Each one is made of a central core—a *nucleus*—surrounded by other tiny bodies called *electrons*. Atoms are not often found on their own. They usually clump together to form bigger groups known as *molecules*. Scientists have learned that the size of the atoms and the number of them that clump together in molecules have a great effect on the way an element reacts.

Since modern chemistry made its first few steps in the eighteenth century it has opened up vast areas of discovery. Those discoveries have in turn founded a great industry which is using its knowledge to push back the frontiers of science.

Below Chemistry is at the forefront of advances in medicine. Operations like this would not be possible without anaesthetics. New drugs can cure diseases that not so long ago were fatal.

(Dulevant—Turin)

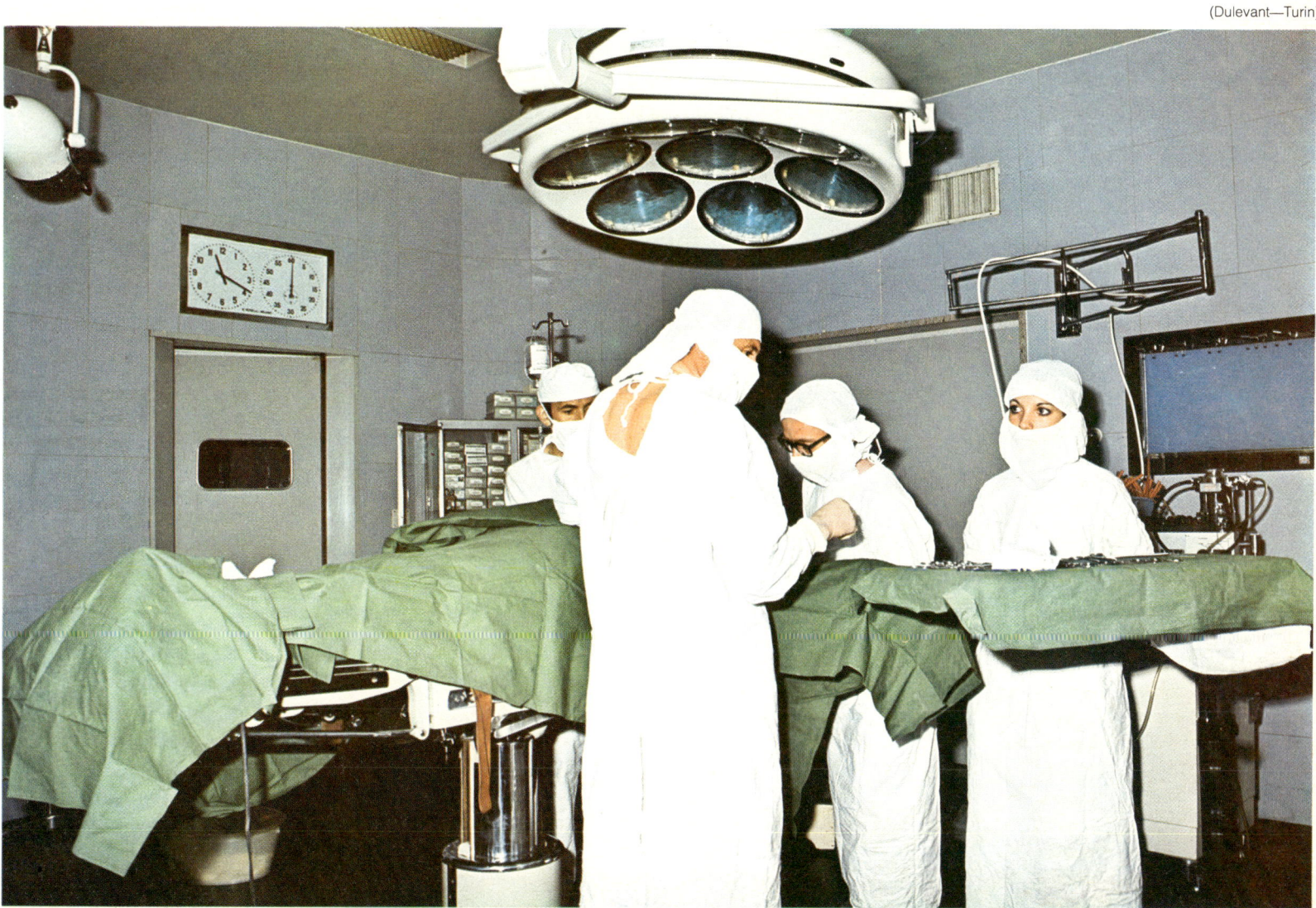

2 Elements and compounds

Chemicals are divided into two categories—elements and compounds. A compound is made up of two or more elements and usually has properties quite different from the elements that make it up.

The elements, in turn, can be divided into two classes, metals and non-metals. Metals in their pure form are usually shiny and range in colour from whitish silver to grey. The exceptions to this are gold and copper which have their own distinctive coloration. The metals are good conductors of heat and electricity and because they are not brittle can be shaped into useful objects. For example, copper can be drawn out or extruded into wire or beaten into shape by hand with hammers. Only one metal—mercury—is a liquid at normal temperatures.

The non-metals have very different properties. They come in a variety of colours and many of them are gases. For example sulphur is a yellow solid while another non-metal, chlorine, is a greenish-coloured gas.

Some elements are unstable and break down to form others while giving off radiation. These are known as *radioactive* elements. And while there are 92 naturally-occurring elements a few others can be artificially made. These are known as the *transuranic* elements and they all share the property of giving off radiation

The elements are divided into metals and non-metals. **Left** Crystalline sulphur, a non-metal. **Below** A gold ingot and a copper pot—both metals. **Right** Nature's abundant supply of elements and compounds can be utilized in many different ways to make our lives richer and healthier. But the world's natural resources must not be abused.

(SEF—Turin)

(SEF—Turin)

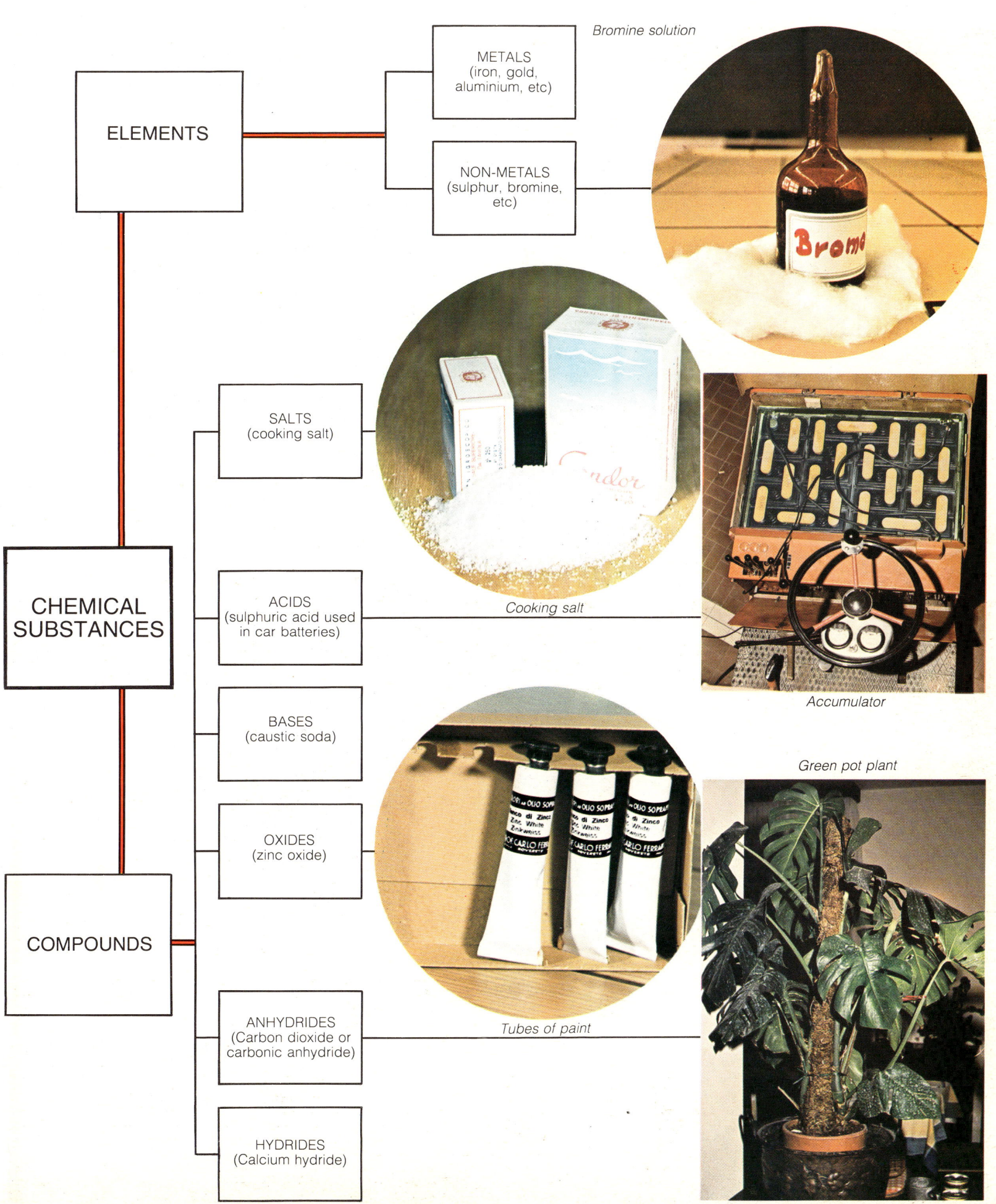

ELEMENTS

METALS
(iron, gold,
aluminium, etc)

NON-METALS
(sulphur, bromine,
etc)

Bromine solution

CHEMICAL
SUBSTANCES

SALTS
(cooking salt)

Cooking salt

ACIDS
(sulphuric acid used
in car batteries)

Accumulator

BASES
(caustic soda)

Green pot plant

OXIDES
(zinc oxide)

COMPOUNDS

ANHYDRIDES
(Carbon dioxide or
carbonic anhydride)

Tubes of paint

HYDRIDES
(Calcium hydride)

| metal +oxygen =oxide | non-metal +oxygen =anhydride |
| oxide +water =base | anhydride +water =acid |

acid +base =salt

Above Farming land can be replenished with vital ingredients by using man-made chemicals or, as shown here, by spreading animal manure.

with uranium and radium. For this reason they are said to be radioactive. Radioactivity was first discovered by the French scientist Becquerel when in 1896 he noticed that uranium gave off radiation. The glow is caused by the radioactive emissions from the element. Marie Curie's discovery of radium in 1898 gave scientists a powerful new tool which has been put to use in curing disease. Radioactive elements are used for generating power from nuclear power stations as well as making nuclear weapons.

The 92 natural elements can be combined in many thousands of ways to make compounds. Among the more simple of these are the *acids* and *bases*.

Acids are usually colourless corrosive liquids which have a sour taste and turn litmus paper red. They have one or more hydrogen atoms in their molecules which may be replaced by metals to form new compounds called *salts*. The best known and strongest acids are hydrochloric, nitric and sulphuric acids.

The bases, also known as *alkalis* or *hydroxides*, are also frequently corrosive. A good example of a strong base is sodium hydroxide which is sold commercially as caustic soda. If a base reacts with an acid it leads to the formation of a salt and water.

The type of salt produced from a simple reaction like this depends upon the sort of acid and base used. But in typical reactions where sodium hydroxide reacts with hydrochloric acid and copper hydroxide reacts with sulphuric acid the products are sodium chloride and copper sulphate respectively. In both reactions water is produced too.

Other common compounds include the *oxides*, sometimes called *anhydrides*, where an element is combined with oxygen. If a metal combines with oxygen it is called a *basic anhydride* because the oxide forms a base when combined with water. But a non-metal combined with oxygen to form an oxide is termed an *acidic anhydride* because it forms an acid when dissolved in water.

Just as many elements can combine with oxygen to make oxides, so many can also combine with hydrogen to form another class of compound called *hydrides*.

So as we have seen it is possible to change one substance into another by chemical reactions. These reactions can take place quickly or slowly depending upon the conditions, and chemists use the properties of chemicals and differences in temperature and pressure to produce the end-product wanted.

The velocity, or rate, of a chemical reaction is also very much affected by the physical state of the chemicals used. For example, iron reacts with oxygen to form an oxide much more quickly when it is a powder than if a large block of iron is used.

Another important type of chemical reaction which is widely used in industry is *electrolysis*. This involves the decomposition of certain compounds in solution by an electric current. These compounds are known as *electro-lytes* and typical reactions occur when they are dissolved in water or when they are in a molten state.

The reason why some liquids will conduct electricity is that the electrolyte molecules break up into charged particles called *ions*. If molecules do not break up into these charged particles they are termed *non-electro-lytes*. It is because the electrolytes were discovered that we are able to extract many metals from ores and to have such useful everyday things as torch batteries.

When the atoms are broken up, or dissociated, in solution, the ions carry a positive or negative charge. The positively-charged ions are called *cations* and the negatively-charged ions are called *anions*.

The branch of chemistry which deals with the conversion of chemical energy into electrical energy and vice versa is called *electrochemistry*. A good example of an electrochemical reaction occurs in a car battery where a chemical reaction produces the electric current to drive the car. Such a battery can be recharged by passing an electric current through it to restore the energy.

Below Some crystals that occur naturally: above left: pink rhodochrosite; above right: green malachite; below left: black ilmenite; below right: yellow citrine quartz.

3 Crystals

Chemists have known for a long time that substances appear naturally in various forms. The earth's crust is made up of *minerals*—vast quantities of the substances that we study in the laboratory as compounds.

For example, calcium carbonate that we commonly know as chalk also appears naturally as limestone and marble. The reason for the differences between these different forms of the same chemical is the way in which they were formed. The conditions of high temperature and immense pressures that forced the rock formations into the shapes that we can see today also had an effect on the structure of the individual molecules within the minerals. Because of these differences in conditions, marble is a crystalline compound where the internal arrangement of the atoms is always regular and conforms to a set pattern. But chalk, although composed of the same atoms, has an unstructured internal arrangement. These unstructured arrangements of molecules are termed *amorphous*, or shapeless, structures.

Crystals can be formed in several different ways. A simple example can be demonstrated by dissolving cooking salt in water and evaporating it. Crystals of salt are left in the bottom of the pan. Crystallization has important uses for the chemist both in the laboratory and in industry. In the laboratory, crystallization at set temperatures can help ensure that the product of a reaction is pure. Sulphur is often purified industrially by a form of crystallizing called *sublimation*. The crude sulphur is heated and becomes a gas which is passed over a cool surface. The pure crystals reform on the cool surface and they can then be scraped off.

Scientists have managed to determine the exact internal structures of many crystals by X-ray photography. This in turn has told us much about the forces that hold the atoms together in crystals. For example, the discovery that the atoms in common salt crystals are regularly spaced in a box-like lattice arrangement held together by relatively strong forces explains why the crystals have a very high melting point. A lot of energy is needed to disrupt the regular arrangement of the atoms before salt will melt.

Crystals can appear singly or as groups and the groupings fall into many different arrangements. Sometimes crystals form too close together to allow a clearly defined pattern. Formations in which it is impossible to pick out individual crystals clearly are *aggregates*.

For ease of study it is convenient to classify crystals into nine distinct systems. And for the same reason chemistry as a whole has been broken down into two main sections. The chemistry of carbon is usually considered separately and this is known as *organic* chemistry. The chemistry of the metals and non-metals apart from carbon is called *inorganic* chemistry.

All types of crystals obey a set of definite laws that govern the shapes that they take. **Above right** Chemists have identified nine different crystal systems. These are: (1) an asymetrical octahedron; (2) and (3) monometric systems; (4) a trigonal scalenohedron; (5) a rhombic bipyramid; (6) a tetragonal disphenoid; (7) a monoclinic prism; (8) a monoclinic system; and (9) a rhombohedral system. Crystals can appear singly or in groups that fall into many different arrangements. The laws which govern crystal shape lead to the formation of crystals like smoky quartz (**above left**), green tourmaline (**below**), and crystals of gold (**below right**).

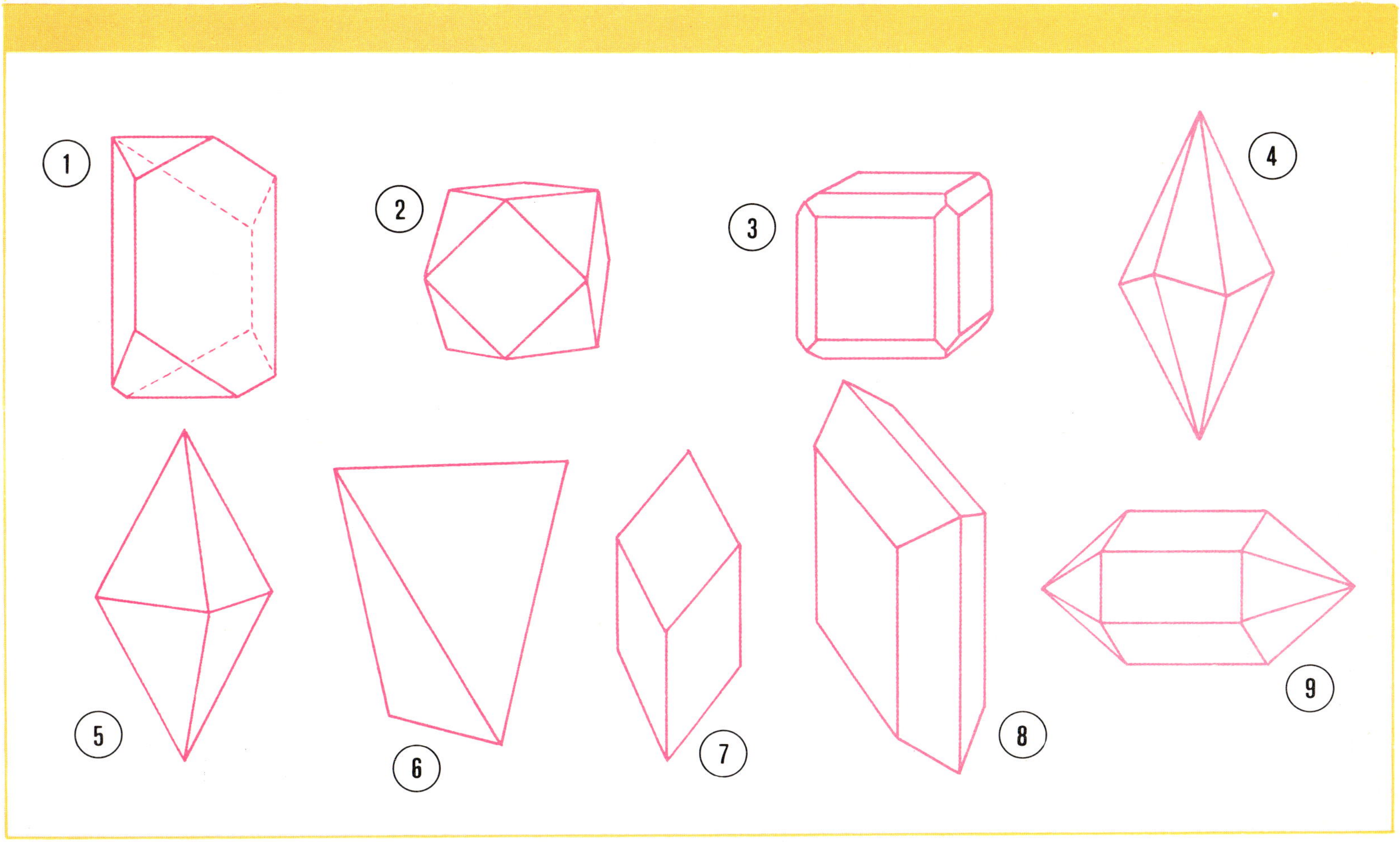
1
2
3
4
5
6
7
8
9

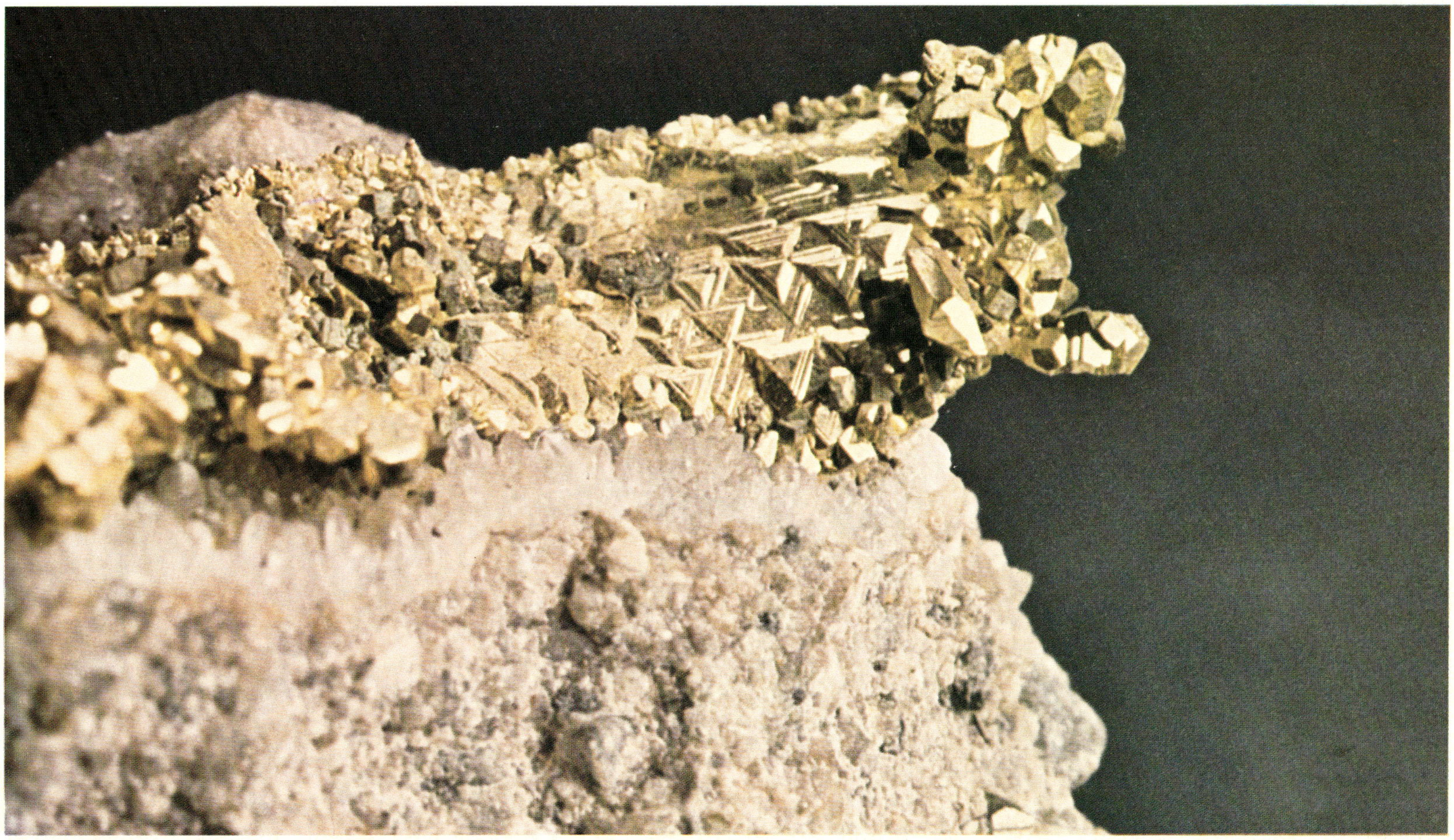

4 Inorganic chemistry

Inorganic chemistry is the study of the elements and their compounds with the exclusion of carbon compounds. For the sake of convenience, the reactions of carbon as an element are usually considered under inorganic chemistry, but the chemistry of its highly complex compounds justifies a whole branch of the science to themselves known as organic chemistry (see Chapter 5).

As we have noted already, one of the most important advances has been the orderly arrangement of the elements into nine groups by the Russian chemist Mendeleev. His Periodic Table (see page 69) enabled scientists to see that elements in the various groups had similar properties and to predict the properties of those still undiscovered. Now that all the gaps have been

(SEF—Turin)

Below A compressed mixture of helium and oxygen enables deep-sea divers to breathe under water.
Inset A photograph taken through a telescope of a solar flare, probably caused by an eruption of burning hydrogen from the surface of the sun.

(Fiore—Turin)

filled in, it is possible to see that his theory was extremely accurate. The elements fall into nine groups where the members all have related properties. It was Mendeleev's belief in his theory that enabled him to predict with confidence—and as it turned out very accurately—exactly what the chemical properties of the missing elements should be and even what they would look like in the pure form. He maintained, for example, that another element would be found to fill the gap between calcium and titanium. He was right.

He based the table on increasing atomic weights, starting with the lightest element of all, hydrogen. Reading down the groups, it is easy to see that the individual members of a group have related properties. Reading across the table, it is possible to subdivide it

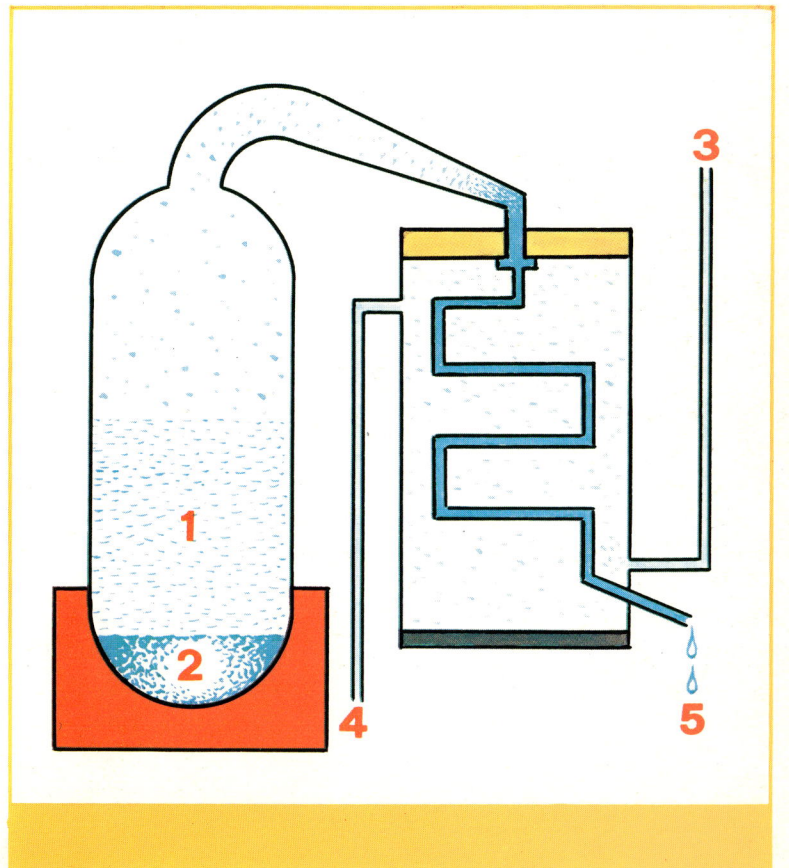

Above Spa water is said to have health-giving properties. All natural water contains dissolved chemicals, usually salts of sodium, potassium, magnesium or calcium. But for some chemical processes it is necessary to have pure water. This is obtained through a process called distillation (**right**). The impure water (1) is left to settle so that any solids (2) fall to the bottom. The water is boiled and the vapour allowed to condense in a spiral tube which is kept cool by water passing over its surface from (3) to (4). The distilled water is collected at the outlet (5).

into periods so that the cross reference is in terms of the increasing weight of the atoms.

The lightest of all the elements is hydrogen. It is lightest because it has the smallest atom with only one proton making up the positively charged nucleus and one electron as the corresponding negative charge. It occurs naturally in the air in very small quantities as a colourless and odourless gas although vast quantities of it are to be found on earth combined with other elements. For example every molecule of water has two hydrogen atoms combined with one of oxygen and hydrogen atoms make up vital constituents of acids, alkalis and all organic substances. These include oil, plastics, coal and proteins. Outside the atmosphere, free hydrogen is found in larger quantities. It makes up a large part of the sun where it is involved in the 'nuclear furnace' processes which give us the warmth and heat that enables life to go on.

Hydrogen is also an important industrial element being used as a welding gas and in the manufacture of various other chemicals. But more and more it is being realized that hydrogen is a very versatile fuel. At the moment, most of our hydrogen needs can be served by extracting it from natural gas. But as the fossil fuels such as oil and coal become more rare, nuclear power and cheaper electricity may make it an attractive alternative to obtain hydrogen by the electrolytic breakdown of water.

Oxygen, of course, is freely available in the air and altogether makes up one-fifth of the atmosphere. It is the commonest element on the face of the earth being combined in most minerals. For industrial purposes, it is extracted by liquifying air. This produces a deep blue liquid which is stored in cylinders and has many uses.

Unlike hydrogen, oxygen does not burn itself but it does support combustion. Each molecule of oxygen is made up of two atoms, but it can exist in another form—or *allotrope*—where three oxygen atoms combine to form a gas called ozone. Ozone is very rare in the air but small quantities are formed by electric sparks such as those produced by electric trains.

The ability of oxygen to form allotropes is closely followed by another member of its family, the familiar element sulphur. Sulphur can exist in several different forms depending mainly upon the amount of heat that it is subjected to. This was one of the similarities of properties which lead Mendeleev to state his Periodic theory of the elements. If we look at one of sulphur's neighbours in the next group of the table we also see allotropes being formed. This element is phosphorus which can exist as white phosphorus or in the red form commonly used in matches, thus bearing out again

Mendeleev's theory of the elements.

We already know that vast amounts of hydrogen are combined with oxygen in water. Water shows just how different a compound can be in chemical and physical properties from the elements that make it up. In its normal state water is a liquid and, indeed, covers three-quarters of the earth's surface. If it is frozen it forms ice, a different physical form which is less dense and floats on water. If it is boiled it forms a vapour which condenses on cooling to reform the liquid. But the most important chemical property of water is that it is the best solvent known.

Many of the elements react with water. The group which contains lithium, sodium and potassium all react violently with water at ordinary temperatures. If a small piece of sodium is dropped onto a dish of water it

Right Chlorine, a powerful germicide, is used to keep swimming baths clean. The gas is bubbled through the water and dissolves in it.

skates around the surface melting as it goes. These metals are called the *alkali metals* because when they react with water they form alkalis. For example sodium reacts with water to form sodium hydroxide (caustic

Right The halogens are an important family of chemicals. For example, bromine is used in medicine and in making film for cameras. **Below right** Iodine is extracted from seawater. Paraffin or petroleum ether is added to the seawater and mixed (A). The iodine dissolves in the oil leaving iodine-free water which is tapped off from a settling tank (B). The oil/iodine mixture (C) is treated with sodium sulphite to free the oily mixture of iodine (D). This is then tapped off to leave a solution of sodium iodide. Further treatment (E) with sulphuric acid and other chemicals leaves pure iodine. At one time iodine was extracted from seaweed.

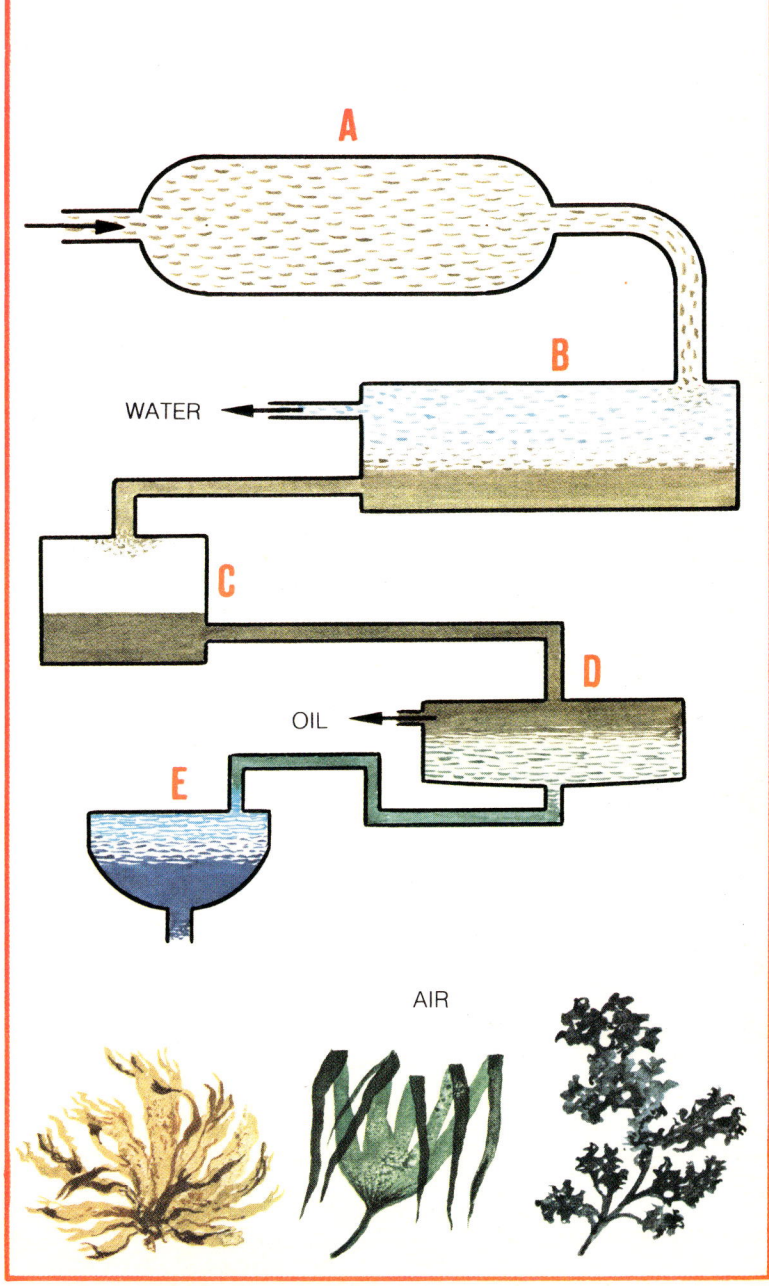

20

soda) and gives off hydrogen in the process.

The next group, called the *alkaline earth metals*, which contains beryllium, magnesium and calcium, react less violently with water, whilst the metals known as the *transition elements*—iron, chromium, cobalt and nickel—react with water only at very high temperatures.

Quite apart from these simple chemical reactions between water and metals, we know that it is absolutely essential for life to exist. Water is rarely found pure and usually contains traces of dissolved salts.

Another group of elements which display very clearly the close relationship of properties between members of the same family are the *halogens*—fluorine, chlorine, bromine, iodine and the radioactive astatine. The first two members of the group are greenish gases while bromine is a brown liquid which gives off fumes; iodine is a violet crystalline solid and astatine occurs naturally only in minute traces.

The first three members of the group all have the same foul choking smell whilst both bromine and iodine are deeply coloured. The halogens are a highly reactive group although their reactivity decreases as the

Above In large vineyards sulphur is often dusted on the vines to protect them from fungal diseases. **Right** Sulphur used to be known as brimstone and is thrown out by volcanoes like this one at Pozzuoli near Naples in Italy.

molecules get bigger over the range from fluorine downwards. For example, where most compounds will not attack glass, fluorine does so readily. When combined with hydrogen to make hydrofluoric acid it is used for glass etching.

Both fluorine and chlorine are manufactured by electrolytic processes. Chlorine is obtained as a by-product during the manufacture of caustic soda from sea water. Although it is a greenish gas at normal temperatures chlorine is easily liquefied and is usually stored as a liquid in cylinders. More than half the industrial output of chlorine is used in the manufacture of other chemicals—notably the well-known plastic PVC (poly-vinyl chloride)—as well as other compounds valuable as solvents, antiseptics, anaesthetics and insecticides.

Chlorine is familiar as a sterilizing agent for drinking water and as a bleaching agent in the production of

(SEF—Turin)

Left Ammonia is one of the most important chemicals in nature and in industry. A lot of it is used as a coolant in refrigerators like this giant cold store. **Below** Very few organisms can fix nitrogen directly from the air although some plants like these peas can do so. **Right** Most plants and animals—which all need nitrogen—have to rely on ammonium compounds, nitrates and nitrites from the soil as their supply. This transfer of nitrogen from the air to the plant and animal kingdoms is called the Nitrogen Cycle. Some plants (A) can covert (fix) nitrogen direct from the air. But all plants absorb nitrogen compounds from the soil too to build up the proteins they need for growth (B). These plants in turn are eaten by animals (C) which return nitrates to the soil through their excreta and when they themselves die and decompose. The complex proteins of animal bodies are broken down by bacteria (D) into simpler chemicals that can be absorbed through plant roots (E). To increase the fertility of the soil we use artificial fertilizers (F). Some nitrogen products are also formed in the air during electrical storms and are carried to the earth dissolved in rain (G).

sulphur is also used to make matches, fireworks, skin ointments and dyes.

The proportion of sulphur dioxide found in the atmosphere is increasing because modern fuels—oil and natural gas—usually contain traces of sulphur. Efforts are being made to treat this pollution by purifying flue gases before they get into the air. When it dissolves in rain water sulphur dioxide forms a weak acid that attacks buildings and corrodes paintwork.

Although sulphur is a poor conductor of electricity, the next member of its group, selenium, has the unusual property of being a good conductor in the light but a poor conductor in the dark. For this reason one of

paper and linen. The chemical industry also uses large amounts for making hydrochloric acid.

Bromine, which is used to make petrol additives and important medical and photographic chemicals, is extracted from sea water by treating it with chlorine. Iodine is obtained from the mineral Chile saltpetre. Iodine is widely used as an antiseptic and because it is essential for healthy growth is often added in small quantities to animal food and table salt.

Sulphur is another important element. Large deposits are found in the United States, Sicile and Japan. The American deposits produce most of the world's supply because it occurs in a relatively pure state there. But large quantities are extracted from ores where sulphur is combined with other elements as sulphides and sulphates.

Sulphur is mainly used for the production of sulphuric acid but it finds large-scale use in the vulcanizing of rubber and as a fungicide in agriculture, particularly for the protection of grape vines. Elemental

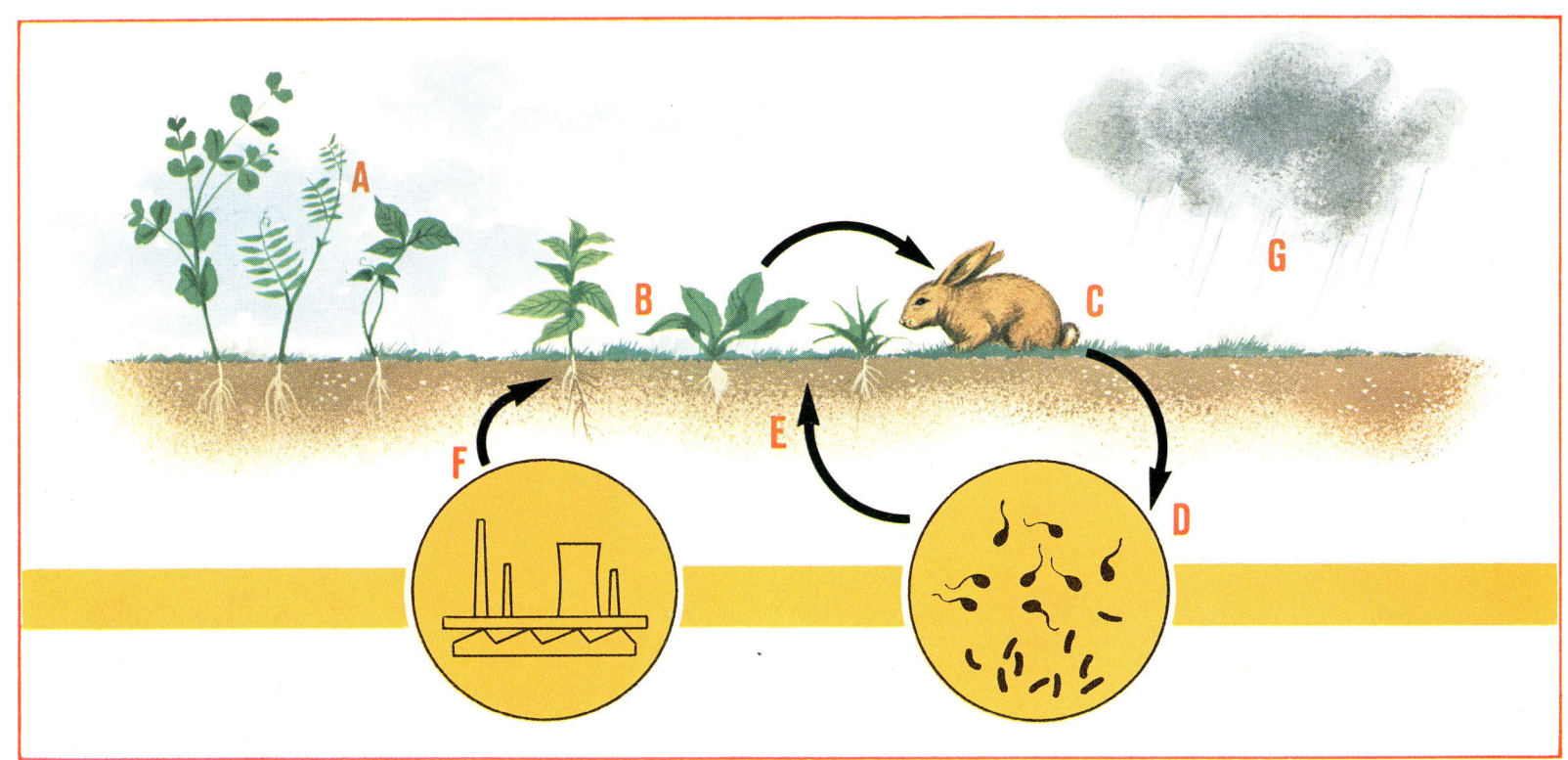

(Dulevant—Turin)

its early applications was in the manufacture of photo-electric cells.

We have seen that oxygen makes up one-fifth of the earth's atmosphere so it is time we looked at the gas that makes up the other four-fifths. This is nitrogen, a colourless, odourless gas. Although there are very few natural deposits of nitrogen compounds, all living things contain large quantities of it because it is an essential part of protein.

Although we obtain nitrogen from the air by liquefying it, most plants and animals cannot do this. For this reason the compounds of nitrogen are vital if it is to be returned to the soil and the plants and work its way back up the chain to animals. One of the most important of the nitrogen compounds in the nitrogen cycle is ammonia. It is made industrially by combining nitrogen with hydrogen in the Haber process and is used mainly to make fertilizers, nitric acid and organic chemicals such as urea and nylon.

Because it is so easily liquefied at room temperature, ammonia is commonly used as a refrigerant in domestic refrigerators and dilute solutions make good cleaning fluids. It is formed naturally by the breakdown of dung and dead animal and plant matter and this is an important source of nitrogen for the soil. Some plants have lumps or nodules on their roots that contain bacteria which can 'fix' nitrogen from the atmosphere. Farmers commonly grow these plants and plough them

Right As we all know, hot air rises. This fact was put to use in the eighteenth century when the hot air balloon was invented.

Above The rare or noble gases neon and argon are used in these luminous electric signs. **Left** Carbon is part of the composition of chalky shells we find on the beach. **Above right** Carbon, like nitrogen, has a natural cycle of its own. Carbon dioxide in the air is formed by combustion (A), the rotting of animal waste in the ground (B), the respiration of land animals (C), natural gases from volcanoes (D), the respiration of marine creatures (E), the decomposition of sea bed deposits (F), and of animal and vegetable deposits on the shore (G). Some carbon dioxide returns to the earth dissolved in rain (H) but most is absorbed from the air by trees and other plants (I) to build up the sugars and starches vital to living things. **Below right** Not all ancient trees were turned into coal. Some like these, in a petrified forest in Arizona, were turned to stone.

back into the soil to ensure a natural supply of nitrogen without using too much expensive fertilizer.

When air is liquefied to produce oxygen and nitrogen, we can see that there are traces of other gases present too. These are a separate group of elements known as the *noble gases*—helium, neon, argon, krypton, xenon and radon.

Helium, the lightest gas known after hydrogen, is used for filling balloons. Although it is not as light as hydrogen, it has the valuable property of being non-inflammable. Mixed with oxygen it is supplied to divers

(Fiore—Turin)

Left If minerals are near the surface they can be scraped away by 'open cast' methods. **Below** Two forms of carbon: a diamond (left) and the graphite used in pencils (right). **Above right** All these are made from clay: bricks, china stoneware and earthenware crockery. **Centre and below right** Some of the beauties of the earth. From the left clockwise: two cut topaz stones, agate, opal, blown glass articles made from sand, and emerald in its natural rock.

who work in pressurized suits because helium is less soluble in the blood than nitrogen. This means that divers can be brought to the surface much quicker and helps to avoid the painful condition known as the bends.

Neon and argon are both used in lighting tubes but few uses have yet been found for krypton and xenon. The last member of the family is the radioactive gas radon. An important use has been found for this noble gas in the treatment of cancer. Because its radioactivity only lasts for about four days, capsules of the gas can be implanted near cancers and the radiation kills the tumour cells.

Phosphorus does not occur freely as an element but most usually as minerals, where it is combined with calcium. The calcium compounds of phosphorus are also found widely in the animal kingdom. These compounds make up much of the enamel on teeth and the hard shanks of bone. Phosphorus can be prepared in three forms: white, red and black. We shall look at the two most important of these forms—or allotropes—white and red phosphorus.

White phosphorus is a waxy substance that catches fire in air. For that reason it is used in incendiary and smoke bombs, but much more is used for making important acids for industry. Red phosphorus, which is made by heating white phosphorus, is used in match heads. Interestingly enough, this reaction can be speeded up by adding a little iodine to the white phosphorus. The iodine acts as a *catalyst*—a substance that alters the rate of the reaction. Usually catalysts are used to speed reactions up.

A far more common element which does appear freely in nature is carbon. It can be found in pure form in

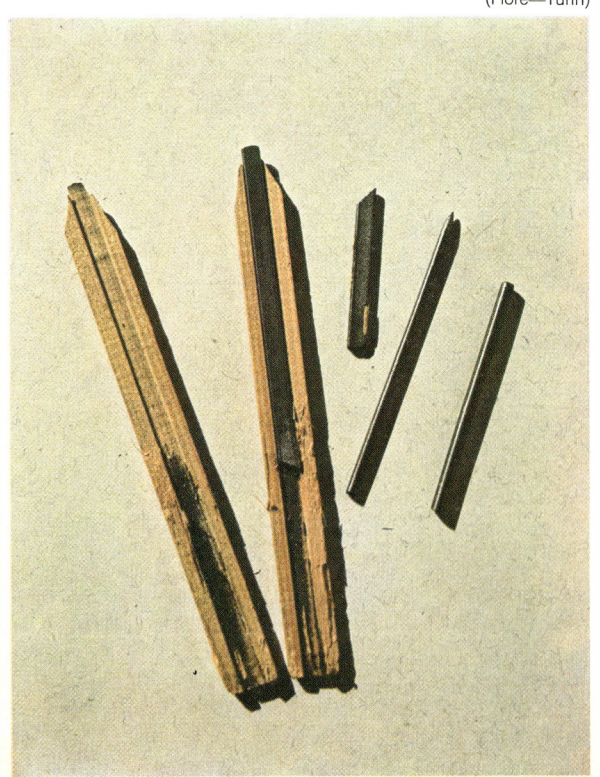

diamonds and graphite. Elsewhere it combines with other elements in the air, soil, plants and animals. Large amounts are found in coal, oil and natural gas where it is often combined with hydrogen to make hydrocarbons. The study of carbon compounds has become so complex that we shall look at them under organic chemistry (see Chapter 5). However, although most carbon compounds come under the heading of organic chemicals there are a few that are of importance to the inorganic chemist. These include the naturally

Jet propulsion by man and nature. **Left** The rocket waits to be fired by the thrust of its jets. **Above** Gas issues from a natural boric acid vent.

occurring pure forms of carbon—diamond and graphite—as well as the gases carbon dioxide, carbon monoxide and the important sulphur compound carbon disulphide. Carbon dioxide finds a wide variety of uses: dissolved in water under pressure it is sold as 'soda water'. Cooled to $-78°C$ it is used as 'dry ice', a solid refrigerant; many fire extinguishers are devices for producing the gas, which puts out fires. A lot of carbon dioxide is used for producing the important organic chemical urea. Another important use is in gas-cooled nuclear reactors where carbon dixoide is used to transfer the heat produced in the atomic pile to steam-raising plant. Carbon dioxide is chosen as the coolant because it causes a very small amount of corrosion to metal containers at high temperatures. Carbon dixode, of course, is produced by the human body and breathed out through the lungs and also forms a vital part of the life cycle of plants. Carbon monoxide, on the other hand, is an extremely poisonous gas which kills quickly in small quantities. It is used principally as a fuel or in the manufacture of synthetic petrol.

At one time it was thought that another important element, silicon, existed in two forms, but recent studies have shown that this is not so. And now that industry has been able to produce very pure forms of silicon its vital use in the electronics industry has been realized. A hard, grey solid in pure form, silicon is the second most common element in the earth's crust and usually occurs combined with oxygen as silica. Silica and the silicates are found in many minerals, rocks, sand and clay.

Some of the natural forms of silica are extremely beautiful. It forms topaz, opal, agate and onyx but it is the impurities which give these gem stones their characteristic colours, not the silica itself. Pure silicon, much of which is used to make the silicon chips that are used in practically all electronic instruments, is usually extracted from silica and it is also used in the manufacture of glass.

Right Common salt has many uses. It is made into hydrogen peroxide, sodium nitrate for fertilizers, sodium carbonate for washing soda, sodium sulphide used in the leather industry, sodium sulphate for the glass industry, and caustic soda. **Below** Loading railway trucks at a salt mine.

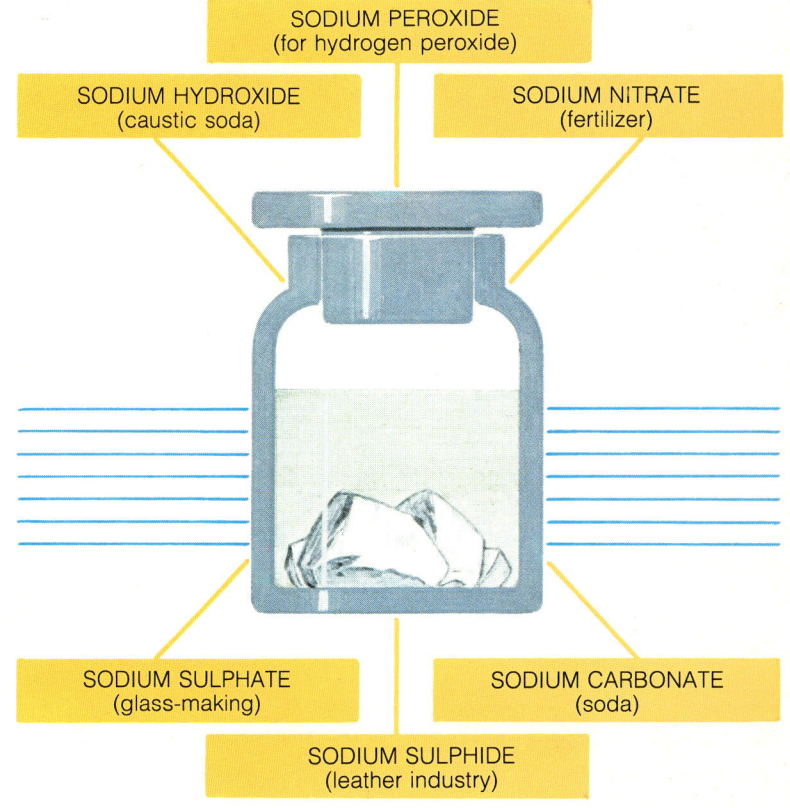

SODIUM PEROXIDE
(for hydrogen peroxide)

SODIUM HYDROXIDE
(caustic soda)

SODIUM NITRATE
(fertilizer)

SODIUM SULPHATE
(glass-making)

SODIUM CARBONATE
(soda)

SODIUM SULPHIDE
(leather industry)

(SEF—Turin)

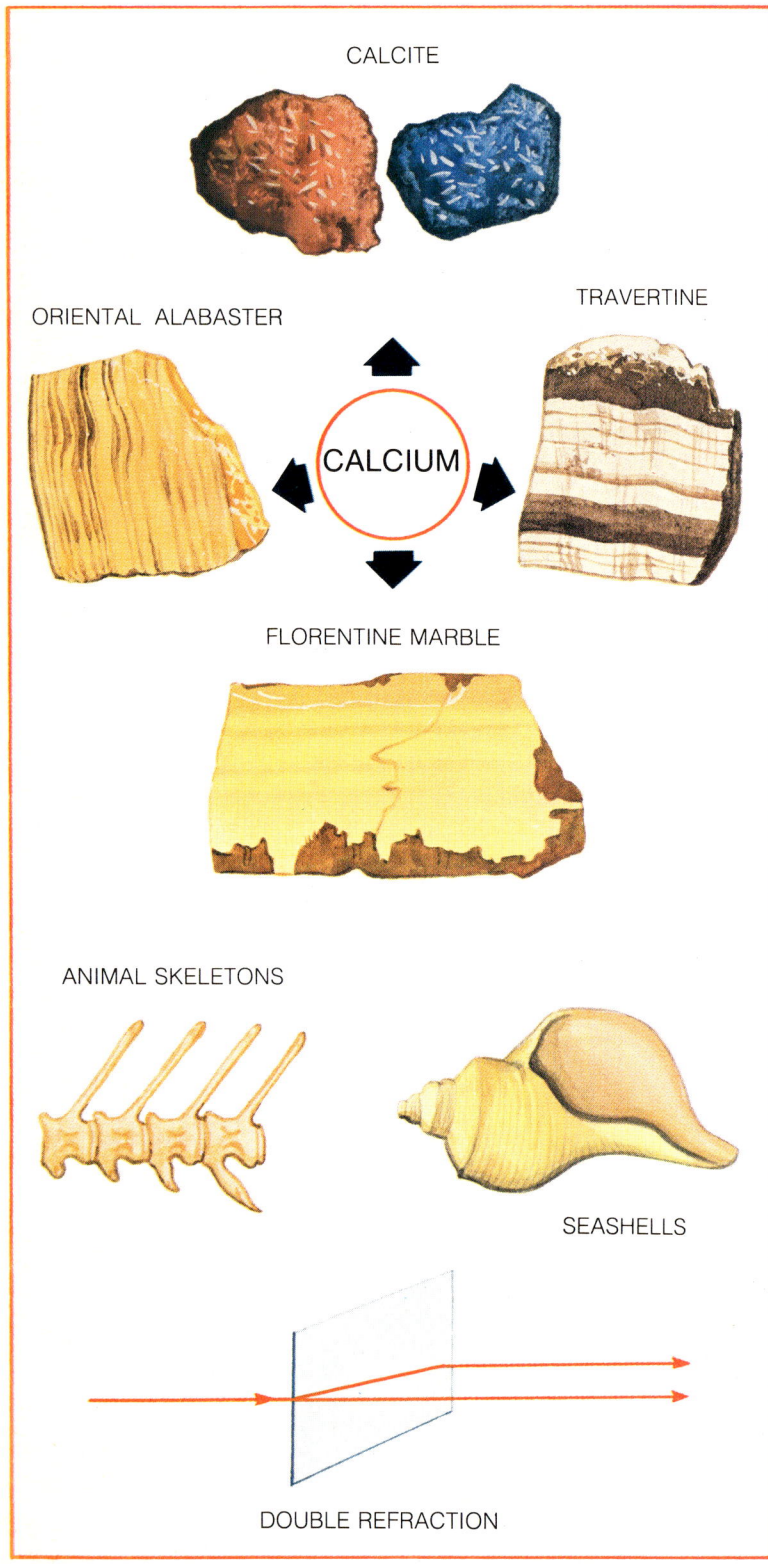

CALCITE

ORIENTAL ALABASTER

TRAVERTINE

CALCIUM

FLORENTINE MARBLE

ANIMAL SKELETONS

SEASHELLS

DOUBLE REFRACTION

from these mediums for use as salt or in the manufacture of soaps.

Calcium is a harder metal than sodium or potassium and is found in huge quantities as chalk and limestone as well as in bones and shells. Calcium products are widely used for making cement, washing soda and quicklime. The third common form of calcium compound found naturally is marble which like chalk and limestone is often white. This is the type most often used by sculptors, but there are many other beautiful colours ranging from black to red through to yellow.

Compounds of the metal barium are commonly used in the paper making industry and in medicine. Because barium compounds are opaque to X-rays, they are used when doctors need to X-ray people's stomachs. This is known as a barium meal, a white tasteless fluid drunk by the patient before the X-ray is carried out.

We shall now look at the group of elements called the metals. Already we have seen that some members of this group, the alkali metals sodium and potassium, react very fiercely with water and for that reason have to be kept in oil. Like many other metals, they are silvery-white and shiny when pure, but they also have the somewhat unusual property of being rather soft as well, and are easily cut with a knife. Neither of these occurs pure naturally. Sodium is most commonly found as sodium chloride—rock salt or brine—and is extracted

While barium compounds are common, those of strontium are not. However both these metals and compounds of potassium and magnesium are used to make fireworks. For example, the different coloured stars in a rocket are made by adding different quantities of metal compounds and every manufacturer keeps his 'recipes' a closely guarded secret. Unfortunately, the most common form of strontium is the radioactive form, strontium-90, which is a product of atomic explosions. In the years when countries freely exploded nuclear

(Pasquali—Bologna)

Below There are giant deposits of calcium in cliffs and mountain ranges such as the Dolomites in Italy. **Right** Traces of metals in fireworks give us different colours. **Below right** Rainwater erodes chalk, another form of calcium carbonate, forming caves as it seeps down. Caves in chalk are usually distinguished by the formation of stalactites and stalagmites.

Above Metal foil is used extensively for packaging. These chocolate eggs are being wrapped in it. **Right** Casting molten copper into ingots.

devices in the atmosphere, quite a lot of it was spread into the air from which it has been absorbed by plants and thus by animals.

Compounds of magnesium, again a silvery-white metal, are very common. Because it is fairly reactive, it does not occur freely in nature, but is commonly found as the rock dolomite. Its compounds are dissolved in seawater and natural springs and it is an essential ingredient of the substance that makes plant leaves green—chlorophyll.

Being soft, magnesium is easily drawn into fine wire and in this form it is used in flash bulbs. When it burns, a brilliant white flame is produced and this property is used both by photographers and by the military to make flares. When combined with other metals in alloys, magnesium forms compounds that are both light and strong. The most common example is when magnesium is combined with aluminium to form magnalium. This is used to make lightweight optical instruments while another alloy—electrum, an alloy of magnesium, aluminium, zinc, copper and manganese—is the light, hard metal used to make engines and aircraft propellers. The powdery white magnesium oxide is sometimes used as a fireproof coating in electric cookers.

Radium is one of the few naturally occurring radioactive elements. In chemical properties and physical appearance it rather resembles barium, but its major characteristic is that it gives off radiation. It is found in trace quantities in uranium ores such as pitchblende in Europe and parts of the Soviet Union or carnotite in the United States and Australia. It is used in radiation therapy for cancer.

Aluminium, the familiar metal of cooking foil and pots and pans, is a light ductile element and a good conductor of electricity. In order to extract the pure metal, bauxite is first of all purified by dissolving it in caustic soda. Most of the impurities are left as a sludge at this stage and filtered off. The remaining solution is further treated to make pure aluminium oxide. The oxide is then dissolved in molten cryolite and the melt is electrolyzed by a huge electric current at a very high temperature.

The metal when extracted is white and lustrous, malleable and ductile and a good conductor of both heat and electricity. For these reasons, it is easily shaped into domestic implements such as cooking pans and increasingly it is being used for making wire to carry electric current.

Apart from the uses already mentioned, aluminium's

weight advantage makes it a very desirable metal for making engines and aircraft panels. Powdered and suspended in oil, it is used as a mirror paint. Industry has also found a way of using the metal's natural tendency to form its own protective layer of oxide. Scientists have found that by using an electrolytic process called anodizing, they can increase the thickness of the layer and at the same time absorb dyes into it, so producing a range of attractive coloured finishes.

Just as aluminium forms a protective layer on the surface, so tin is used to coat cans used for storing food. It has been found that tin does not corrode as easily as other metals so food stays fresh. The tin—which is not poisonous—is plated onto steel either by dipping the plate into molten tin or, more commonly now, by electrolysis. Another use for the metal is in making glass. Scientists found that because it has a comparatively low melting point and is extremely resistant to atmospheric corrosion, a layer of molten glass can be floated on a layer of molten tin. The glass is then allowed to cool giving a surface which is perfectly smooth and needs no polishing or grinding. More recently, biologists have found that tin compounds in toothpaste can help prevent tooth decay.

Tin does not occur naturally, usually being found as the mineral cassiterite or tinstone. It has always been highly valued and some of the deposits first to be mined were in Cornwall where the old workings can still be seen. Nowadays most of the world's supply comes from Bolivia, Malaysia and Indonesia. The pure metal is extracted from the ore by roasting it in a furnace. It is a soft silvery metal and can exist in three forms, grey, white or rhombic, depending on the temperature.

Tin is often combined with another metal, lead, to make solders used in electrical joints. Lead, a soft grey metal, is found in many parts of the world—particularly Australia, the United States and Mexico. The principal ore is galena, lead sulphide, from which the metal is extracted by roasting in a furnace. The crude lead contains many impurities such as copper, zinc, iron, arsenic, antimony, sulphur and silver. Even though there is only a small amount of silver present, it is an important source of the metal and great care is taken to recover it.

Although lead is not strong enough to be made into wire, it is often used for sheathing cables because it is highly resistant to corrosion, very soft and has a low melting point. It used to be used for making water pipes and for roofing, but it has been found that small amounts of lead dissolve into the drinking water and as far as roofing goes, cheaper and lighter materials have been found. However, it still has many modern applica-

steels renowned for hardness and strength. Vanadium compounds are widely used in industry as catalysts while chromium is familiar to all of us as the shiny protective coating plated onto so many metal objects such as car bumpers.

Traces of manganese are necessary for healthy plant growth but industrially the metal is mainly used to make armoured steel which can be forged into plate for tanks and warships or into more domestic objects such as safes. Again, its compounds are often used by chemists as catalysts.

Cobalt is another transition metal that is essential in diet. It is particularly necessary for sheep to have it in their food and cobalt atoms are found in vitamin B12. Industrially, cobalt alloys are used for making permanent magnets and for high-speed cutting tools.

Strength is also a characteristic of nickel steels.

The old and the new: **Below** An antique copper jug. **Left** Copper windings in a modern dynamo.

(SEF—Turin)

tions. Lead is used in car batteries, for making weights and bullets, shot and type metal. Because it is so dense, it is used for screening against radiation and lead containers are often used for transporting highly radioactive isotopes. The chemical industry uses the metal in making petrol additives and for the familiar red lead paint which is highly resistant to corrosion by water.

Titanium is one of a very important group of metals that we shall look at next. These are called the *transition metals* and there are ten of them. This group—scandium, titanium, vanadium, chromium, manganese, iron, cobalt, nickel, copper and zinc—have many properties in common. They are hard, lustrous metals with high melting and boiling points. With the exception of scandium and zinc, they form highly-coloured compounds and chromium, manganese, iron, cobalt and nickel are all magnetic.

Many of the transition metals are used industrially as catalysts to speed up reactions and small quantities are used in steel-making processes to give alloys of great strength and hardness. Titanium, for example, is widely used for the construction of aircraft and missiles because of its great strength and lightness. Its remarkable resistance to attack by seawater is being exploited by boat builders and this property has also found wide application in surgery where it is used to make steel pins that hold broken bones together. The titanium pin remains uncorroded throughout the life of the patient. As we have already seen, the oxide of titanium is used in paints as a pigment but it is also used as a filler for paper, soap, rubber and linoleum.

Vanadium and chromium are both used to make

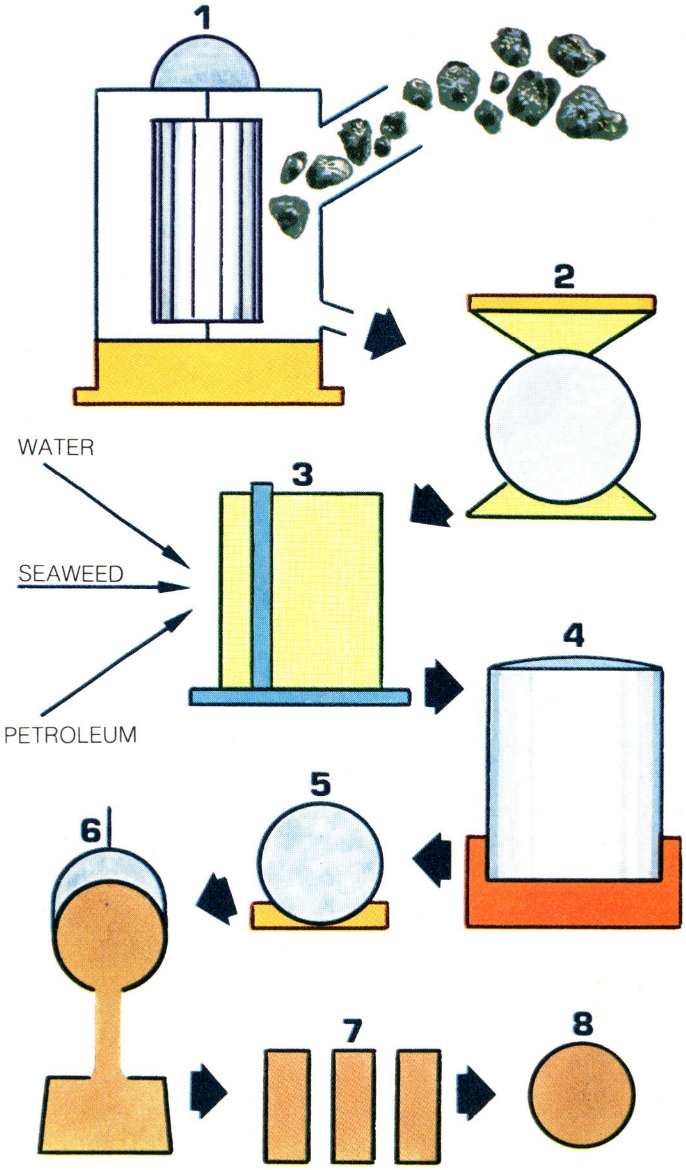

Above An ancient gold ornament. **Right** Extraction of copper from its ores. The ore is first crushed (1) and then powdered in a mill (2). The pulverized ore is mixed with air, water and oil in a flotation chamber where most of the unwanted material is removed (3). The crude ore is smelted (4) and further purified in a converter (5) by a blast of air which takes out all but a tiny proportion of unwanted matter. The metal is cast into ingots (6) and further purified by electrolytic treatment (7). The end product (8) is more than 99.9 per cent copper.

WATER

SEAWEED

PETROLEUM

Natural copper in quartz

Gold in quartz

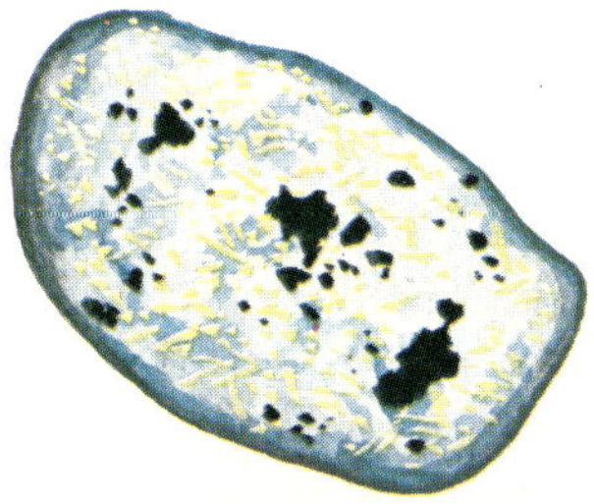

Argentite, a silver ore

Nickel is added to iron to make stainless steel and when alloyed with chromium it is used for making heating elements for electric fires and furnaces.

Having glanced briefly at some of the transition metals, let us now look at the three most important members of the series: iron, copper and zinc. Looking at the Periodic Table we can see that there is a family relationship between copper, silver and gold and zinc, cadmium and mercury, so we can include these four metals in this section too.

Copper, silver and gold are commonly known as the *coinage metals* and are very similar in many respects. For example, all three are so resistant to chemical corrosion that they occur naturally though both copper and silver compounds are mined as ores. They are all highly lustrous and capable of taking a high polish; they melt at about 1,000°C and are excellent conductors of heat and electricity. Silver is the best conductor of electricity known. Chemically, their reactions are similar too. For example, they are all attacked by chlorine and can all form highly coloured compounds. Copper is the most widely used. We find it as wires and utensils, as alloys—brass and bronze—and in plumbing and roofing.

Apart from its own value as a pure metal used in jewellery, silver is widely used as a plated surface and as an industrial catalyst. Silver compounds are particularly important in photography because some of them have the special property of darkening when exposed to light.

Gold—the only metal accepted as currency internationally—is remarkable chemically because it is not attacked by any single acid. It can, however, be made to dissolve in a mixture of acids known as aqua regia. It is used for electroplating cheaper metals, for filling teeth and in photography. If gold is added to molten glass the much-prized ruby glass is made.

Zinc is also used for plating metals to protect them from corrosion. We are all familiar with galvanized iron used for fences and roofing. The process of galvanization is named after the chemist Galvani who invented it. But although zinc plating is widely used, it is never used to plate food tins because it is too poisonous. Some zinc compounds which are not so poisonous are used in cosmetics and creams.

Cadmium is an excellent protector of steel when plated onto the surface and this is one of its main uses. Larger amounts are used now to make compact nickel-cadmium batteries which have a very long life.

Mercury, the only liquid metal, finds many uses in industry and the laboratory. It is used for filling thermometers and barometers and its property of combining with other metals to form amalgams is used in dentistry for tooth filling. Its highly poisonous vapour is used in intensely bright mercury vapour lights.

Probably the most important member of the transition metal group is iron. It does not occur pure naturally—unless you count the iron found in fallen meteorites—but its compounds are very common. Iron is essential for life on earth because it is the centre of red

Below Some of the many articles made from metals. **Above right** The World War II battleship *North Carolina*. Thousands of tonnes of different sorts of steel went into her. **Below right** The earth is sometimes considered as having four layers: a core made mainly of iron and nickel, a sima layer of silicon and magnesium, a magma layer of silicon and aluminium, and the crust containing all the elements.

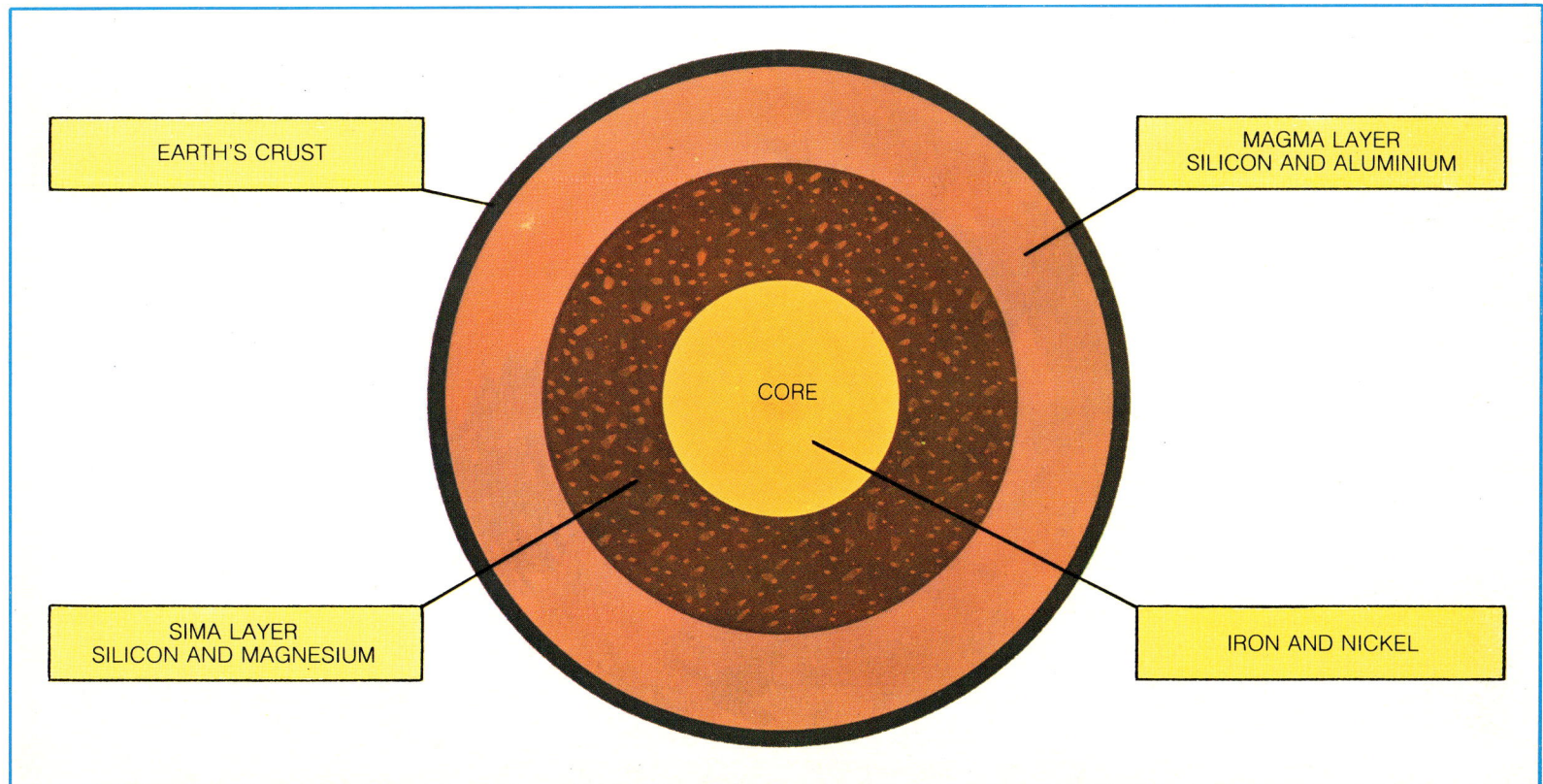

EARTH'S CRUST

MAGMA LAYER
SILICON AND ALUMINIUM

CORE

SIMA LAYER
SILICON AND MAGNESIUM

IRON AND NICKEL

(SEF—Turin)

Uses of iron and steel. **Left** A richly decorated wrought iron gate near Buckingham Palace. **Above** A suspension bridge supported by giant steel cables in New York. **Right** Casting molten metal in an iron foundry.

blood cells and chlorophyll in plants.

Pure iron is produced from the ores by smelting in a blast furnace with coke. As the iron melts and runs to the bottom of the furnace, it is tapped off and run into moulds. But at this stage the iron—which is known as *pig iron*—is far from pure. It contains traces of other metals and quite a lot of carbon which makes it very brittle. To purify it, the pig iron is melted and pure oxygen is blown through it.

Cast iron is pig iron mixed with scrap steel and melted before being cast into shapes for things like drain pipes and fire grates where cheapness is more important than strength. Wrought iron, on the other hand, is almost pure. It is soft but very tough and can be easily welded and forged.

Steel is an alloy of carbon and iron with other elements added to give the desired properties. As we have seen, stainless steels contain chromium and sometimes nickel too. But it is not just the chemical properties of steel that are important. The physical strength of a steel is greatly affected by the way in which it is cooled. *Quenching*, as the process is known, can have a

40

Left Discoveries about some non-metals have revolutionized the electronics industry enabling us to make ever smaller circuits like these tiny diodes and transistors. **Below** A nuclear power station. The peaceful use of nuclear power has given us another way of generating electricity.

large effect on the steel's hardness and toughness. There are two main processes for making steel, the Bessemer and Siemens Martin (or open hearth) processes.

Before we leave the metals, we should look briefly at the radioactive metals such as uranium which are having an increasingly large importance in our lives because of nuclear power. All the radioactive metals have been discovered and isolated within the last 100 years and only a few are of major importance. Uranium, of course, is used in nuclear bombs and reactors and another metal which can be produced from uranium—plutonium—is also of increasing importance. It is the energy of the particles emitting radioactive substances that enables us to use them for industrial and medical purposes as well as in warfare.

5 Organic chemistry

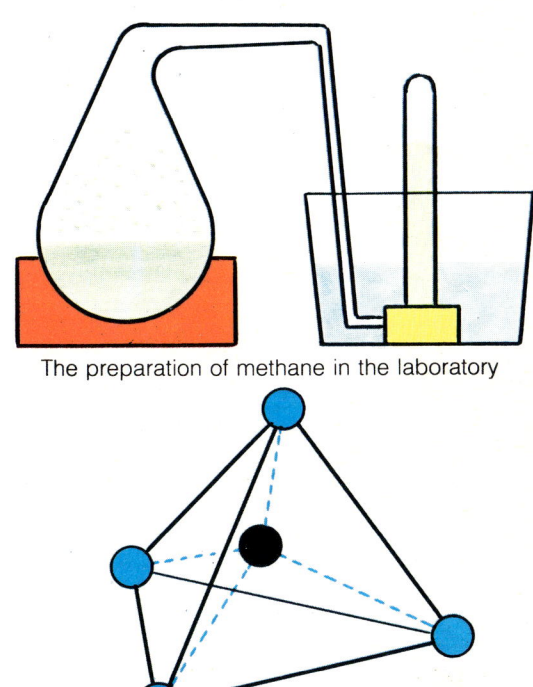

The preparation of methane in the laboratory

The structural formula of methane

(Titus—Turin)

In the early days the term 'organic chemical' was applied only to substances of plant or animal origin. The name was taken from their association with living organisms. Chemicals such as fats, sugars and alcohols were thought to differ from those that we have already looked at under the heading inorganic chemistry. They were thought to have a mysterious vital force which made it impossible for man to prepare them from purely inorganic materials.

But in the early years of the last century the chemists of the day got a shock. For in 1828 the German chemist Wohler prepared urea, which was quite indisputably organic, from the equally indisputably inorganic chemical ammonium cyanate. Wohler prepared his ammonium cyanate from inorganic materials and broke the spell that had made a difference between organic and inorganic chemistry.

The new theory took a little time to catch on, but over the next 30 years other preparations of organic chemicals were made from inorganic substances and the vital force theory fell into disuse. However, the name organic chemistry was retained much as a matter of convenience as it was slowly realized that it was, in fact, the chemistry of carbon compounds.

Above left Natural gas, which consists mainly of methane, is transported along pipelines. **Above right** Methane, the simplest organic compound, is made up of one atom of carbon surrounded by four atoms of hydrogen. Its chemical formula is CH_4. **Right** Vast amounts of carbon are tied up in the chalk which forms the white cliffs of Dover.

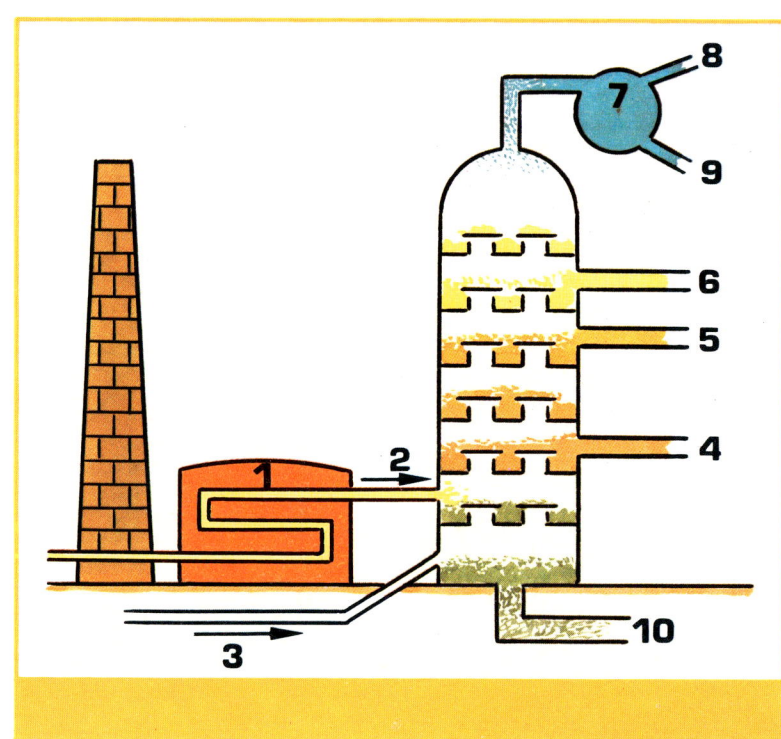

Apart from a very few, which as we have seen are studied under the heading of inorganic chemistry such as carbon's oxides, carbon compounds are grouped together under this heading as a separate branch of chemistry because of the features they have in common and because many of them are of great medical and biochemical interest.

The total number of organic compounds is vast. They far outnumber the sum total of the possible combinations of all the other elements added together. Since the early days, more than four million separate organic compounds have been identified. But it is a striking feature of this branch of chemistry that so few elements are involved in making up the huge number of compounds.

Carbon, of course, is always present. So usually is hydrogen. Compounds composed of the two elements alone are called hydrocarbons. There are many thousands of them including such important substances as methane, ethylene, acetylene, benzene and toluene.

Many organic compounds contain oxygen as well, and sometimes the halogens—fluorine, chlorine and bromine—are present as well as nitrogen. Compounds containing metals, phosphorus and sulphur are occasionally encountered but other elements are rare in organic chemistry.

So basically three elements, carbon, hydrogen and oxygen, can combine to form many thousands—if not millions—of different chemicals. Why is this? The answer to the question lies in the ability of the carbon atom to form stable compounds in either a ring or a straight chain form.

The straight chain compounds are known as *aliphatic*

Above left When crude oil is heated it separates into very definite parts, or fractions, that boil at set temperatures. The lightest fractions are the gases which are stored as liquids under pressure in cylinders. **Above right** The crude oil is first of all heated so that it boils into vapour (1). The vapour (2) is passed into the separating or fractionating tower which is heated by steam (3). The stream of vapour carries the lightest components—those with the lowest boiling point—up to the top of the tower. The heavier ones are left at lower levels. The heaviest are the lubricating oils (4), followed by fuel oils (5). The mixture of hydrocarbons that make up petrol come next (6) and the gases are collected by a condenser at the top (7). The useful gases, (8 and 9) are condensed under pressure and stored. Waste is removed (10).

compounds while the ring compounds are usually known as *aromatic compounds*. There are a few compounds that research has shown to have carbon rings in their make-up that do not have the same characteristics as the aromatics, but they are few by comparison with the aromatics. These are called *alicyclic compounds*.

Carbon can form chains and rings of great size and complexity and no other element has this ability to anything like the same extent. It is this above all else that we must remember about carbon. For example, where hydrogen has an atomic weight of one, some carbon compounds—particularly the proteins—can reach weights of 60,000 to 80,000. In some chemicals, called carbohydrates, the weights of the molecules can go even higher. The reason is the ability of carbon, which we so often see as charcoal or graphite in pencils, to form these enormous molecules that are stable. In fact, carbon combines with hydrogen, oxygen, nitrogen and the halogens with almost equal ease.

Most organic chemicals are extremely volatile—this means that they boil at low temperatures, for the most part below 300°C. In general, they do not conduct electricity and do not mix easily with water. An example of this can be found if whisky, gin or vodka are mixed with water. They all contain ethyl alcohol, a common organic chemical. Wavy lines will appear in the glass and you won't be able to see through it as well as you could through a glass of water where an inorganic chemical, such as salt, has been dissolved. Chemists refer to this unmixability as *immiscibility* and it is generally characteristic of organic chemicals. However, organic chemicals often dissolve easily in solvents like benzene.

This difference in *solubility* (the ability to dissolve) has very important practical consequences. Preparations of organic chemicals usually take longer to dissolve than inorganic chemicals because of their complicated structure and relative inactivity. For example, their preparation often take heating and thorough mixing (heat speeds up chemical reactions).

Because it is possible to make so many different chemicals from the same number of carbon and hydrogen atoms, it is misleading to consider organic chemicals in terms of just the total number of each in the molecule. Many organic chemicals have the same number of atoms of each element in their make-up but are totally different. This phenomenon is called *isomerism*. Chemists define isomerism as the state where two or more different compounds can exist having the same molecular formula (the same number of each atom of different element in the molecule) but with different arrangements of their atoms in the molecule.

Most organic chemicals are inflammable and burn in air. Indeed, most of our fuels are organic—coal, wood, petrol, oil and natural gas—and their combustion gives us our main sources of power. Beside our consumption of these fuels, nuclear power makes only a small contribution because these fossil fuels, as they are known, are cheap and easy to handle.

Generally speaking, if the proportion of carbon in an organic chemical is high, it burns with a smoky flame. Thus if you burn rubber which contains a very high carbon proportion it produces dense clouds of black smoke which can settle as a sooty carbon deposit. When coal was the most popular fuel in use, especially

Below Crude oil is usually forced out of the ground by natural pressure. But when this dies away, engineers set up pumping stations to force it up.

towards the end of the last century and the early years of this one, buildings were coated with a similar sooty deposit that in many towns we can still see today.

The amount of visible smoke in the air has been cut down too by the increasing use of natural gas. This is mostly made up of the gas methane, which occurs as marsh gas and the dreaded and explosive fire damp in badly-ventilated coal mines.

Methane is a good example of a simple aliphatic organic compound. Its chemical formula is CH_4, being made of one carbon atom surrounded by four hydrogen atoms. It is the first member of what is probably the most important family of organic chemicals, the paraffins, or alkanes. The next three members are ethane, C_2H_6, and the gases commonly used as a fuel in cigarette lighters, propane and butane, C_3H_8 and C_4H_{10} respectively. Calor Gas, used extensively for heating and cooking in caravans, is made up almost entirely of propane. We thus see how aliphatic compounds start to build up into chains. The carbon atoms in the molecules mentioned above are linked in chains with the hydrogen atoms arranged around them.

The aromatic organic chemicals are distinguished by features that separate them from aliphatic chemicals that contain the same number of atoms in their molecules. Because of the characteristic ring structure of aromatic compounds like benzene, they usually have

a higher boiling point than comparable chain structures and most of them are solids or liquids.

The six-carbon benzene ring is the basis of all aromatic carbon compounds and it is a very stable structure. It is so strong that it can persist unbroken through a whole series of chemical reactions involving other groups that are attached to it.

We can now see that not only is chemistry divided into two main parts, inorganic and organic, but also that organic chemistry is itself split into two, aliphatic and aromatic organic chemistry. Let us start back at the beginning with aliphatic chemistry, the study of the straight chain compounds of carbon.

There are three basic groups of aliphatic chemicals that we have to look at in organic chemistry. First, as we know, there are the alkanes or paraffins with their first member being methane. Second come the alkenes or olefins whose first representative is the very important chemical ethylene. Third are the alkynes and the first member of the family here is acetylene.

The main source of methane is natural gas. It can also be obtained from coal gas of which it makes up about 40 per cent and from sewage. It is a clean fuel, burning in air to form water and carbon dioxide, and this is its main use. The chemical industry uses methane not only as a fuel but also as a source of such substances as the dry-cleaning fluid carbon tetrachloride, hydrogen, carbon black (a very pure fine form of carbon), acetylene, methyl chloride, carbon disulphide and hydrocyanic acid.

All of the members of the alkane family are colourless and have no smell—something that makes methane very dangerous in coal mines where a slight spark can cause a massive blast. Before the invention of the Davy lamp and, more recently, the electric lamp, miners had to carry a canary in a cage when they went down a mine. They held the unfortunate bird above their heads and if it died they could be sure that there was fire damp about because methane is lighter than air and floats above it.

This is a convenient point to have a look at the refining of crude oil since it is mostly made up of a mixture of alkanes. Crude oil is an evil-smelling dark coloured thick liquid found in huge deposits under the earth mainly in the Middle East, but also in the United States, Canada and under the bed of the North Sea and in some South American countries and the USSR. It is thought to have been formed by the action of bacteria on plant and animal remains under high pressure, but its

exact origin remains uncertain.

The composition of the oil varies with its country of origin, but crude oil is usually made up of a mixture of paraffins, containing carbon chains of anything from one to 40 per molecule, along with some olefins (alkenes) and other groups called cycloparaffins (or naphthenes) and aromatic hydrocarbons. There are often organic sulphur compounds present as well which generally have to be removed during processing.

Crude oil is such a complex mixture that any given

(Dulevant—Turin)

Left and above Both film and gramophone records are made possible by the plastics industry which uses chemicals produced from oil and coal.

sample may contain over 100 compounds, most of them liquids at room temperature, with gases dissolved in them. One of the great values of crude oil from Saudi Arabia is that it contains practically no sulphur at all, and is therefore much easier and cheaper to process.

The crude oil is extracted by drilling holes into the ground, often many thousands of metres deep, and letting the oil flow up under its own pressure. When that pressure eases, it may be necessary to draw up the residue with pumps. After separating out any solids and the dissolved gases the crude oil is broken up into various portions known as *fractions*. This is achieved by heating the crude oil to about four times boiling point and passing the vapours up a tall tower called a fractionating tower. Here, depending upon their boiling points, they condense at various layers. This is the first stage in the process of refining the crude oil.

The fractions can then be distilled again to separate the useful fractions even further. For example, to get the petrol which we use in cars, the naphtha fraction is treated to give a whole range of chemicals which all boil at low temperatures. Petrol is made of this mixture of organic compounds but in fact makes up only a small part of the total yield of organic chemicals from crude oil.

Usually, when oil is discovered, natural gas is there too lying as a layer above the oil. To speed up the extraction of oil from the earth, many oil companies used to burn this gas off—the process is called flaring—but economic pressures have forced them to realize that natural gas is very valuable as a fuel.

As crude oil and natural gas become more expensive, chemists are casting their eyes around for cheaper sources of fuel, either natural or synthetic. They have come to the conclusion that with prices rising so rapidly, coal may be the answer to the fuel crisis. Western Europe, the United States and the USSR all have vast coal deposits. During World War II when natural petrol was in short supply, the Germans successfully operated synthetic fuel plants based on coal and it seems likely that this solution may be adopted in the future.

The most important of the alkene family is ethylene, which has a two carbon chain with four hydrogen atoms attached to it. Its formula is C_2H_4.

Right Both formic and acetic acid are widely used in industry. Formic acid is used in dyeing (A), alcohols (B), and tanning (C); from acetic acid we get aspirin (D), acetone (E), mineral water (F) and vinegar (G). It is also used in the manufacture of dyes (H) and artificial silk (I) and for waterproofing fabrics (J).
Below Fruit and vegetables are improved in quality by the use of chemicals.

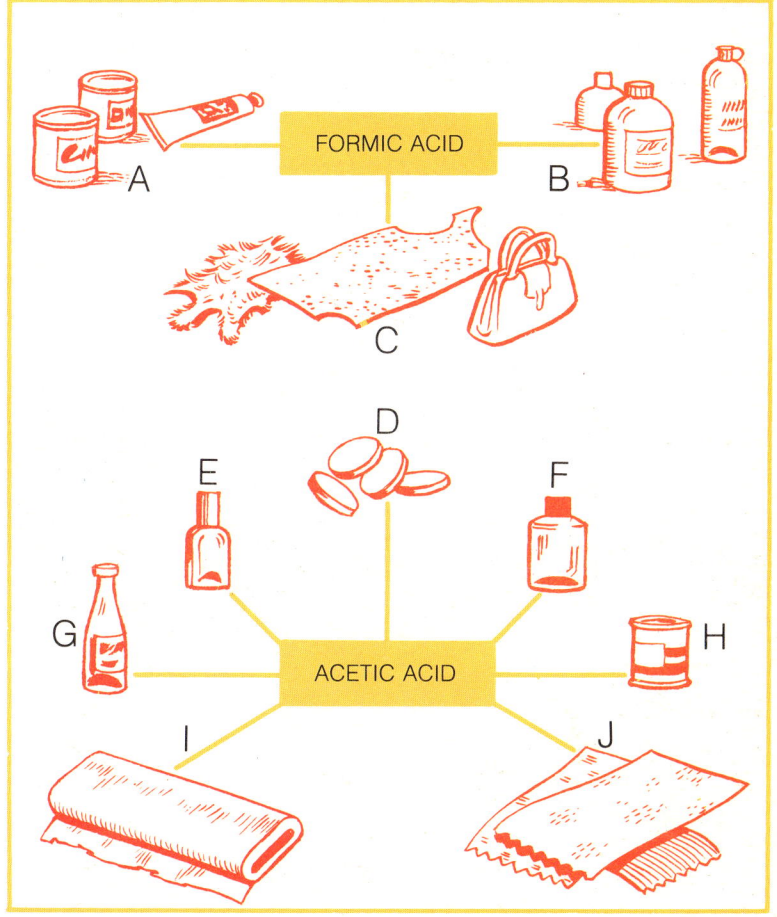

Oranges, lemons and grapefruit are all bigger and better because of chemical discoveries.

As we might expect, the alkenes are colourless gases. This corresponds to the similarity in their general formula to the group we have just looked at, the alkanes. But there is one difference. They all have a sweetish smell. The most important of the family, without any doubt, is ethylene. This gas, which is produced mainly by cracking crude oil, is used in vast quantities to manufacture the common plastic, polythene. Polythene is tough, light, easily moulded and dyed, is a very good insulator and extremely resistant to attack by acids and alkalis. All these properties are useful from a chemist's point of view, but it is equally hard to break down once the useful life of an article made from it is over.

A lot of ethylene is converted into another chemical

called styrene which in turn is converted in to another common plastic, polystyrene, or mixed with butadiene to make synthetic rubber. But that really is only the beginning for ethylene. It is probably the most useful source chemical obtained from crude oil and is used to make ethyl alcohol, antifreeze, detergents, acetic acid, petrol additives, another plastic called polyvinyl-chloride (PVC) and the important industrial chemical, ethylene dibromide.

The next member of the family, propylene, is almost as important for the chemical industry. It too is extracted from crude oil and is used to make synthetic fibres, polyester resins, acetone and phenol—them-selves important industrial organic chemicals—cyclo-propane (a well known anaesthetic), as well as solvents and detergents. The synthetic fibres made from propy-lene are used in clothes, ropes and fishing nets.

Acetylene, the representative member of the alkyne

family, is a colourless and almost odourless gas which burns very well in air. For this reason, it is often used mixed with pure oxygen in oxyacetylene torches where the high temperature produced will cut through most steels. But most of the acetylene produced industrially is used to make another chemical, acetaldehyde, which

Right Fats and natural oils will not mix with water. If an oil (1) is mixed with water (2) it floats on top. But if the same oil (3) is mixed with an organic solvent (4) it dissolves completely. Fats like tallow and butter are usually solid (5) while oils (e.g. olive oil) are usually liquid at ordinary temperatures (6). Light alters them (7). If they are heated (8) they discolour because new organic compounds are formed. One of the major uses of fats and oils is in soap making. Fats and oils (A) are combined with caustic soda (B) in a tank kept at a steady boiling temperature by an element (C). Salt is added to solidify, or precipitate, the soap which is led off as a liquid (D). The residues are drawn off (E).

5 6 7 8

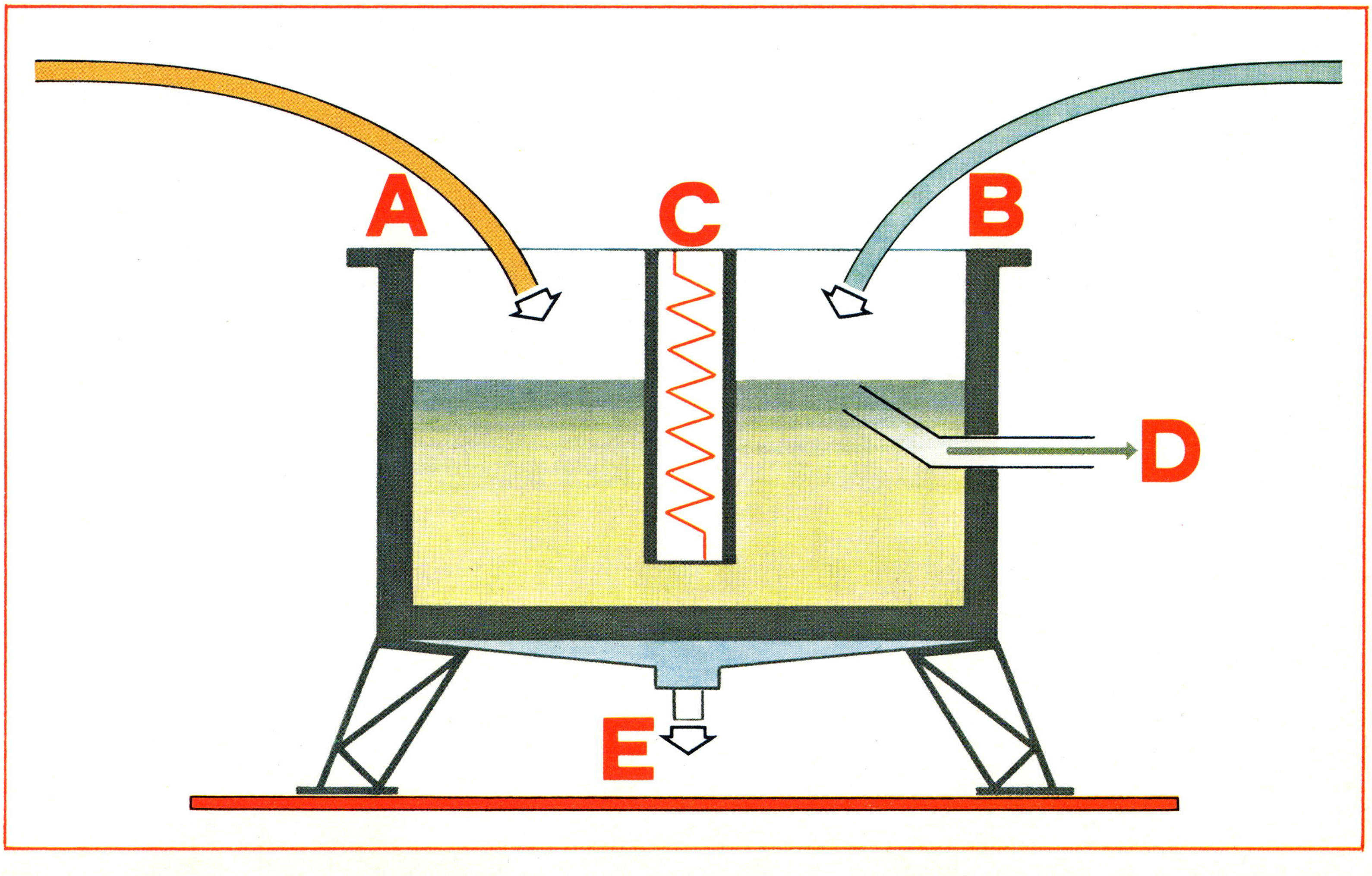

A C B D E

Left Bees make natural waxes to build their honeycombs. Another natural organic chemical is used in papermaking. This is cellulose found in the trunks of the trees stacked outside a papermill (**below**) and in trees like these larches seen in their autumn colours (**right**).

is then used to manufacture other chemicals including plastics and drugs. Some acetylene is used in making PVC and even more in making the synthetic rubber, neoprene, which is often made into diving suits for frogmen. Another use for acetylene in the synthetic fibre industry has been found too. It is the starting chemical for the common synthetic yarns sold under the trade names Acrilan, Orlon and Courtelle.

The next group we shall look at are the alcohols. The most common of these, naturally, is the well-known ethyl alcohol that is present in all alcoholic beverages such as beer and wine. The alcohol family can be regarded as being derived from the alkanes by the replacement of hydrogen atoms with hydroxyl(OH) groups. Thus where the formula for ethane is C_6H_6, the formula for ethyl alcohol is C_6H_5OH.

A colourless fluid, like the rest of the alcohols, ethyl alcohol is widely used as a solvent for resins, varnishes, soaps, perfumes, dyes, and drugs. It is used to make many other organic chemicals, particularly acetaldehyde, chloral and chloroform. As a fuel it is used neat or mixed with petrol in racing cars and with the growing shortage of fossil fuels is already being sold

Above Organic chemicals give these apricots their smell and flavour. **Below left** Other organic chemicals make the distinctive colouring of the scarlet ibis.

mixed with petrol to ordinary motorists in the United States. Because it has a low freezing point, it is sometimes used as an antifreeze and for thermometers.

Its neighbour, methyl alcohol, is sometimes called wood alcohol because that was the original source from which it was made. Large amounts of it are converted to formaldehyde and other compounds from which plastics like Perspex are made.

Both alcohols are increasingly being produced by the fermentation of plants like sugar beet which have a high sugar content and are sometimes sold mixed as the familiar solvent, methylated spirits, or meths.

Another common alcohol is glycerol, but this has three OH groups in its molecule. It is used extensively for making resins and varnishes which have a hard glossy finish and in cosmetics. Glycerol is sometimes used in the manufacture of explosives.

The next two important aliphatic groups are the aldehydes and ketones. Two most common aldehydes are formaldehyde and acetaldehyde while the most common ketone is acetone. Both groups have the same general formula but the aldehydes have what is called a reactive hydrogen atom which confers slightly different properties on the group. Both groups can be prepared from the alcohols. Acetaldehyde is used for conversion into acetic acid and acetic anhydride and it is also used for making synthetic rubbers. Another product, metaldehyde, is the active ingredient of most slug killers and yet another product, paraldehyde, is a powerful sedative.

Formaldehyde also has a wide range of uses. Mixed

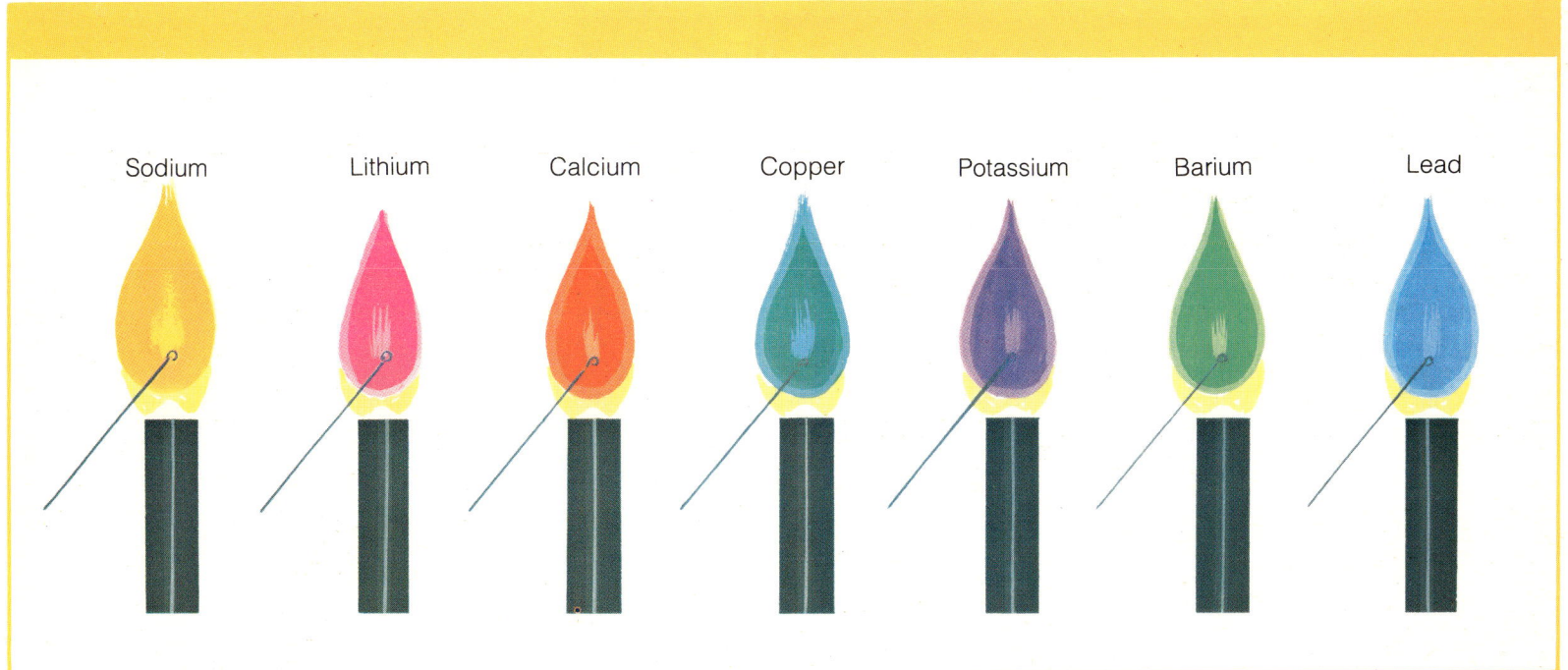

Sodium   Lithium   Calcium   Copper   Potassium   Barium   Lead

with water it is the powerful preservative and disinfectant, formalin. It can also be used for making adhesives and was used in the first plastic to be manufactured on a wide scale—Bakelite. Treated with concentrated nitric acid, formaldehyde makes the powerful explosive, cyclonite, commonly known as RDX. Acetone, too, finds ready use in the explosives industry. It is used to dissolve acetylene, guncotton, nitroglycerine, cellulose acetate rayon, celluloid, lacquers and varnishes of all kinds and is the starting point for the manufacture of chloroform.

Analysis is the major tool of the chemist trying to find out what things are made of. **Above** we see the distinctive colours made by metals in a flame and **below** a typical analytical chemical laboratory.

The organic acids all contain the carboxyl group (COOH) in their molecular make-up and we shall look at one of the most common of the aliphatic acids—acetic acid. Usually prepared from ethyl alcohol, acetic acid is widely used in the manufacture of cellulose acetate where it is used to treat cotton waste. The product is used in packaging and making cigarette filters. Acetic

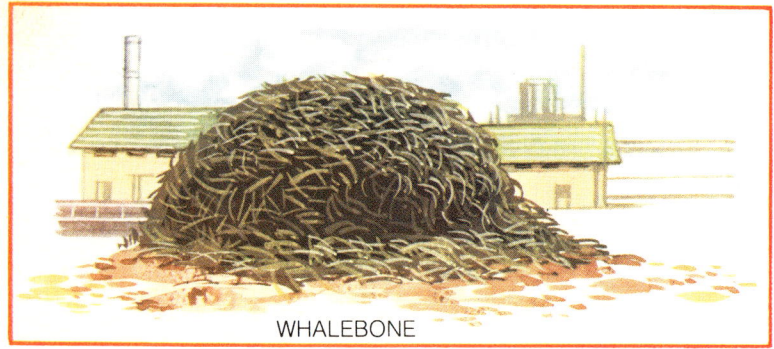

WHALEBONE

APATITE

DUNGHILL

PEATMOSS

Above Some sources of fertilizers. **Right** Grazing cattle provide both meat and natural fertilizer through their dung.

leaves of rhubarb, is often used for stripping old varnish off wood and industrially it crops up in the manufacture of printing inks and metal polishes.

When an acid and an alcohol react together they form a new compound called an *ester*, and also some water. For example, if ethyl alcohol and acetic acid react, ethyl acetate and water are formed. This simple ester is commonly used as a solvent in products like nail varnish, but the importance of the group as a whole cannot be underestimated. Esters have a characteristic sweetish smell and all fats and oils of animal or vegetable origin fall into the group. They are all esters of the alcohol glycerol and a sharp distinction should be drawn here between these oils and fats and those produced from mineral oil.

A good example of an ester is the product formed from glycerol and the fatty acid, palmitic acid. Apart from the palmitates, other common esters are the stearates and oleates. A complex organic ester is usually a

acid plays a part in making acetate rayon for clothes, for making other organic chemicals and, as vinegar, for flavouring and preserving food.

Its neighbour in the family, formic acid, is used industrially for tanning and textile processing as well as for coagulating rubber latex. Formic acid occurs naturally as the substance which stings in stinging nettles and as the irritant in some insect bites. Oxalic acid, which can be found naturally in the poisonous

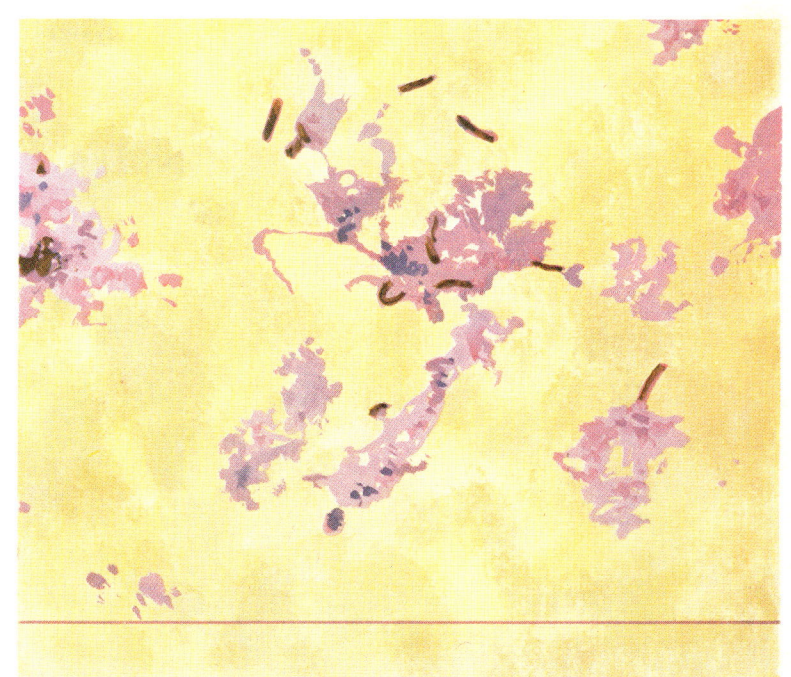

mixture of different glycerides (glycerol compounds) and they find many uses in our society. For example, both soap and margarine are made from them.

Natural fats are used mainly for food and account for up to half the energy content of the human diet. Apart from soap making, the esters are the major source of supply for making glycerol and waxes for candles and greases.

Soaps are the sodium and potassium salts of palmitic, oleic and stearic acids. They are made by boiling acids for long periods with sodium or potassium hydroxide until the conversion is complete. The soap settles out when a solution of common salt is added. The soap is collected and the mixture of glycerol, salt and water is

(SEF—Turin)

(Fiore—Turin)

run off. Both the salt and the glycerol can be recovered from this mixture. In areas where there is hard water—water which contains many dissolved inorganic salts—washing produces a scum on the water and not very much foam. The scum is made up of the calcium salts of the stearates, oleates and palmitates which are insoluble. In recent years, soap has had severe competition from detergents which have the advantage that they retain their washing efficiency even in hard water.

Detergents are usually made from the products of mineral oil cracking such as the sulphur compounds of benzene. But even though detergents have taken a large part of the cleansing market we still need soap as an everyday cleaning agent. The way they work is quite interesting. As we have seen, soaps have long carbon chains which mix easily with the greasy base that makes up most of the dirt on clothes and skin. But they

also have an inorganic ion, sodium or potassium, which links well with water. The result is almost what could be described as a 'chemical bridge' between the dirt and the water with the result that the dirt particles are dragged away from the clothes into the water. This process is hastened by the physical process of scrubbing or agitation in the washing machine.

The fluoride derivatives of the alkanes are particularly interesting because of the great strength of the link between the tiny fluorine atom and the relatively large organic molecule. This means that they are very stable and unreactive. For this reason, they are often used as refrigerants, particularly where large quantities of such a compound are needed. A good example is a freezer ship where the cold store capacity outstrips most refrigeration plants on land.

Organic compounds which contain nitrogen are called

amines. They are important to us because the body contains many amino acids—also nitrogen containing—which when put together make up the proteins that make up most of the human body. Usually we absorb these from food, but several can be synthesized by the body itself through complex reactions inside our cells. The smaller amines have some importance in chemistry, however. They are used to make a wide range of products including weedkillers, insecticides, detergents, dyes and drugs and include the important chemical urea, which you will remember, was the very first organic chemical to be made in the laboratory. The modern uses of urea include fertilizers, glues, plastics and drugs, the most important of which is probably making phenobarbitone, the sleeping drug.

As we have seen, amino acids are derived from the amines and so are another vital biological group of chemicals, the nucleic acids, which carry our inherited characteristics from generation to generation. These giant molecules are called DNA and RNA.

Another of these vital classes of organic compounds are the carbohydrates which we take into our bodies by eating foods like sugar and bread. They are divided into two classes, the crystalline carbohydrates which dis-

Left Many organic and inorganic chemicals are used in the leather industry for curing raw hides and producing different finishes. **Right** The fur trade also uses chemicals for treating skins. **Below** The expansion of the organic chemical industry has given us many new adhesives and glues.

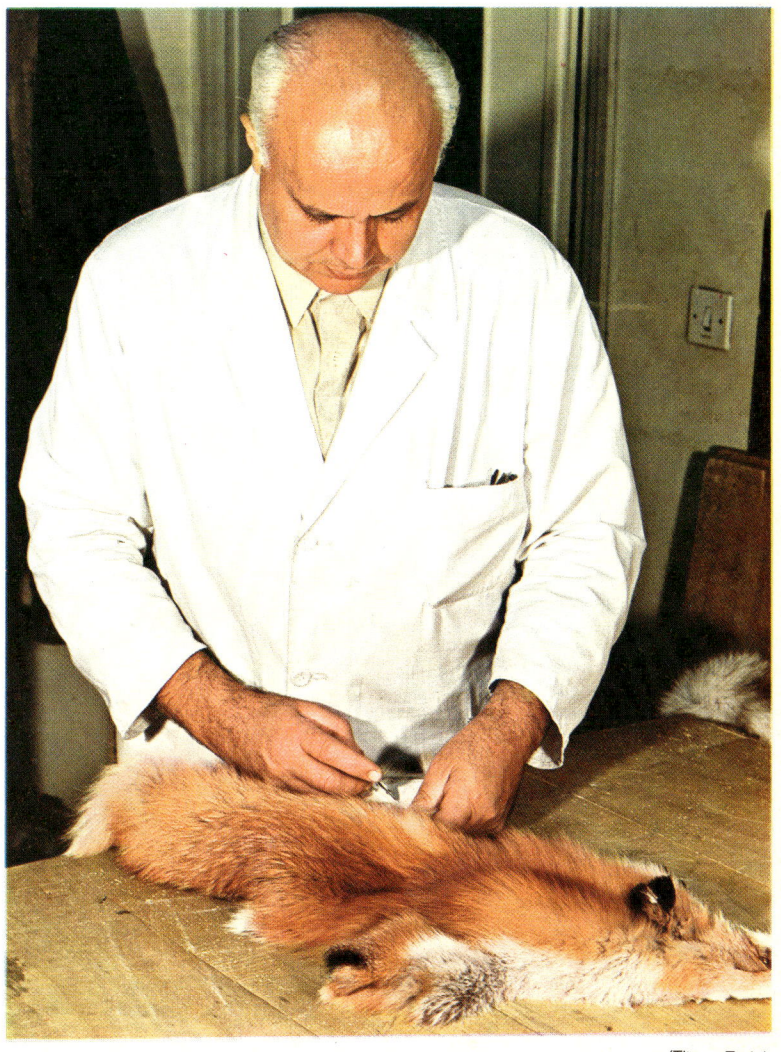

(Titus—Turin)

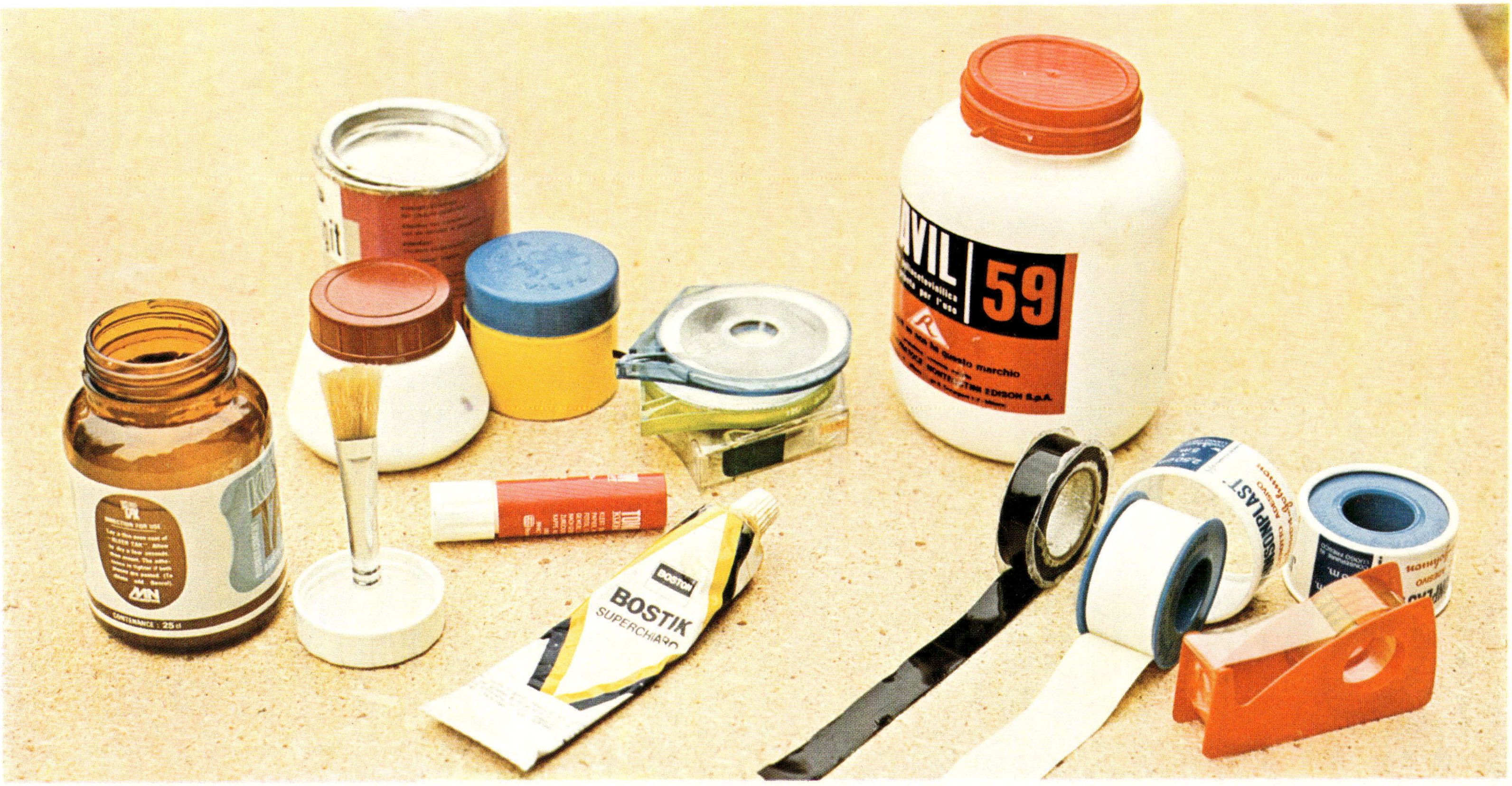

(SEF—Turin)

Above Only a small proportion of synthetic detergents are used for such domestic appliances as the washing machine. Many of the different types of detergents manufactured are used in industry. They may be inorganic, such as those based on carbonate and bicarbonate of soda, or they may be natural organic substances, such as saponins (obtained from plants), used in the manufacture of toothpastes and shampoos. Synthetic detergents produce a great deal of foam. They are sometimes used to good effect along sea coasts to counteract or reduce the harm done by invading oil slicks.

solve in water and have a sweet taste, such as glucose, and the non-crystalline which are insoluble and almost tasteless, such as flour. All of them, however, contain carbon, hydrogen and oxygen. In the body, carbohydrates are used as sugars to give us energy or stored as starch. Another important member of the group is cellulose which makes up the rigid cell walls of plants. We can use this as food although a more important use of cellulose is in the making of fibres and yarns. We can use cellulose this way because it is not a very reactive chemical. The body absorbs sugars and starch much more easily than cellulose and most of it passes out unchanged. And if it is treated with the right chemicals, cellulose can be converted into the familiar plastic wrapping, cellophane. Treated with acids, cellulose forms guncotton which in turn is used to make cordite, the propellant in bullets and shells, and gelignite, a powerful explosive.

The aromatic, or ring compounds are generally made from coal or petrol and the basic unit is the six-carbon benzene ring. Benzene itself is very useful, being the

starting point for the manufacture of a whole range of other chemicals and products such as synthetic rubber, detergents, phenol (carbolic acid), aniline (from which dyes are made), the insecticide DDT and nylon, to name but a few. It also dissolves a wide range of compounds easily such as fats, oils, resins, sulphur, iodine and rubber.

Combined with nitrogen, a whole new range of benzene compounds is revealed. Nitrobenzene, which has the smell of almonds, is used to make aniline for dyes. Another benzene derivative, toluene, is used to make the explosive trinitrotoluene, more usually known as TNT.

The other main benzene compound is phenol, also known as carbolic acid. The characteristic smell is the same as in carbolic soap. Indeed, many antiseptics

Below When industrial chemical wastes are released unchecked from factories and processing plants, they can pollute rivers and streams and cause untold damage to man's natural surroundings.

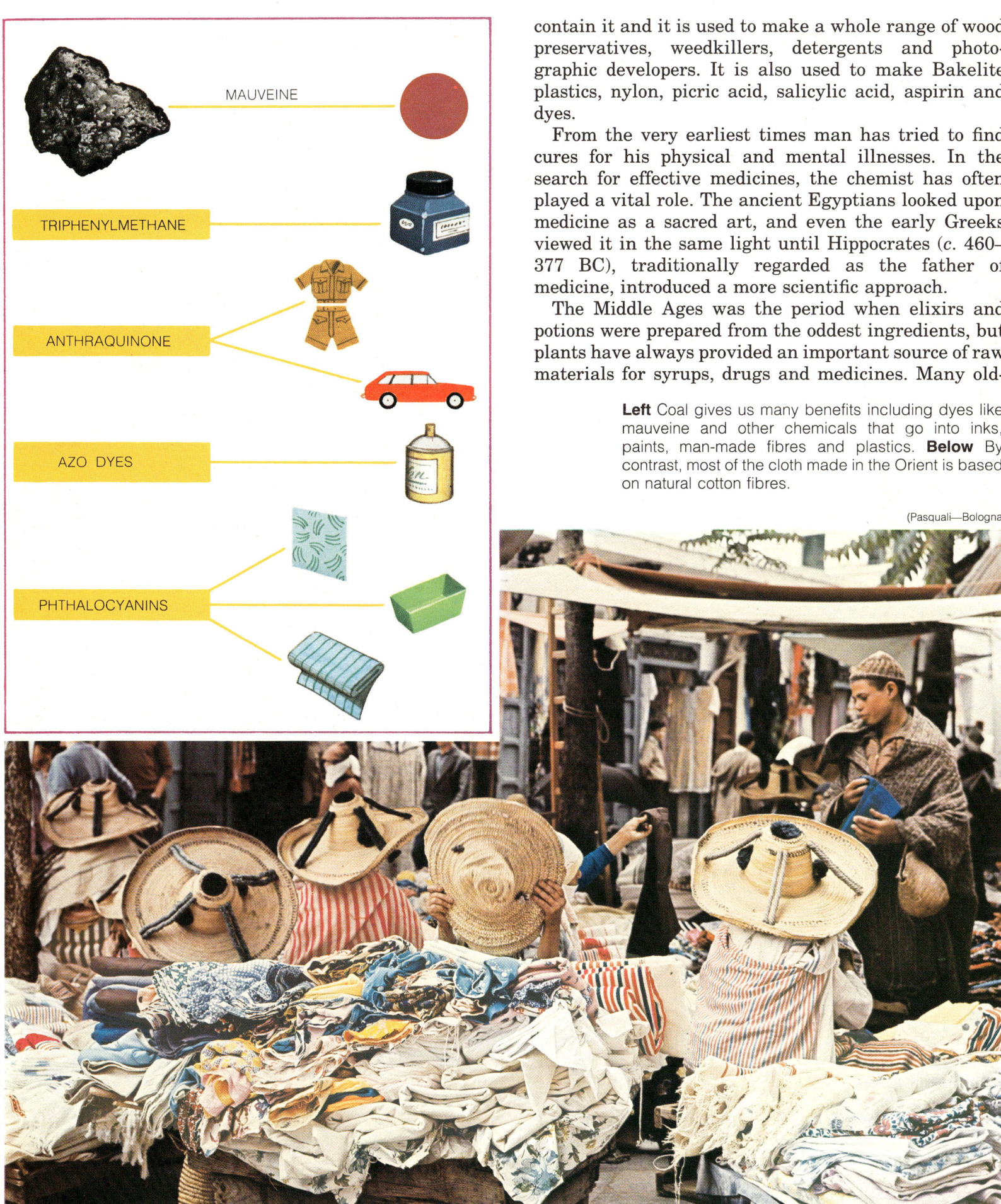

MAUVEINE

TRIPHENYLMETHANE

ANTHRAQUINONE

AZO DYES

PHTHALOCYANINS

contain it and it is used to make a whole range of wood preservatives, weedkillers, detergents and photographic developers. It is also used to make Bakelite plastics, nylon, picric acid, salicylic acid, aspirin and dyes.

From the very earliest times man has tried to find cures for his physical and mental illnesses. In the search for effective medicines, the chemist has often played a vital role. The ancient Egyptians looked upon medicine as a sacred art, and even the early Greeks viewed it in the same light until Hippocrates (c. 460–377 BC), traditionally regarded as the father of medicine, introduced a more scientific approach.

The Middle Ages was the period when elixirs and potions were prepared from the oddest ingredients, but plants have always provided an important source of raw materials for syrups, drugs and medicines. Many old-

Left Coal gives us many benefits including dyes like mauveine and other chemicals that go into inks, paints, man-made fibres and plastics. **Below** By contrast, most of the cloth made in the Orient is based on natural cotton fibres.

(Pasquali—Bologna)

Left and below We wouldn't have plastic utensils without the chemical industry. Neither would Niki Lauda have been able to drive his Ferrari. **Right** Chemical research helps us to control plants. There are growth inhibitors (A), cell poisons (B), defoliants (C), and chemicals which make dwarf plants (D). To protect plants we use fungicides (E), ground disinfectants (F), seed disinfectants (G), fruit preservatives and ripeners (H), and chemicals that protect natural fibres like rope and leather (I). Selective weedkillers are used in rice fields (L), on canal banks (M), and on cereals (N), sugar (O), tomatoes (P) and cotton (Q).

age remedies have been proved by modern chemists to be extremely effective and a great number of medicinal plants and herbs are still regarded as such today and are used in medicine and in other branches of the

(Attualfoto—Bologna)

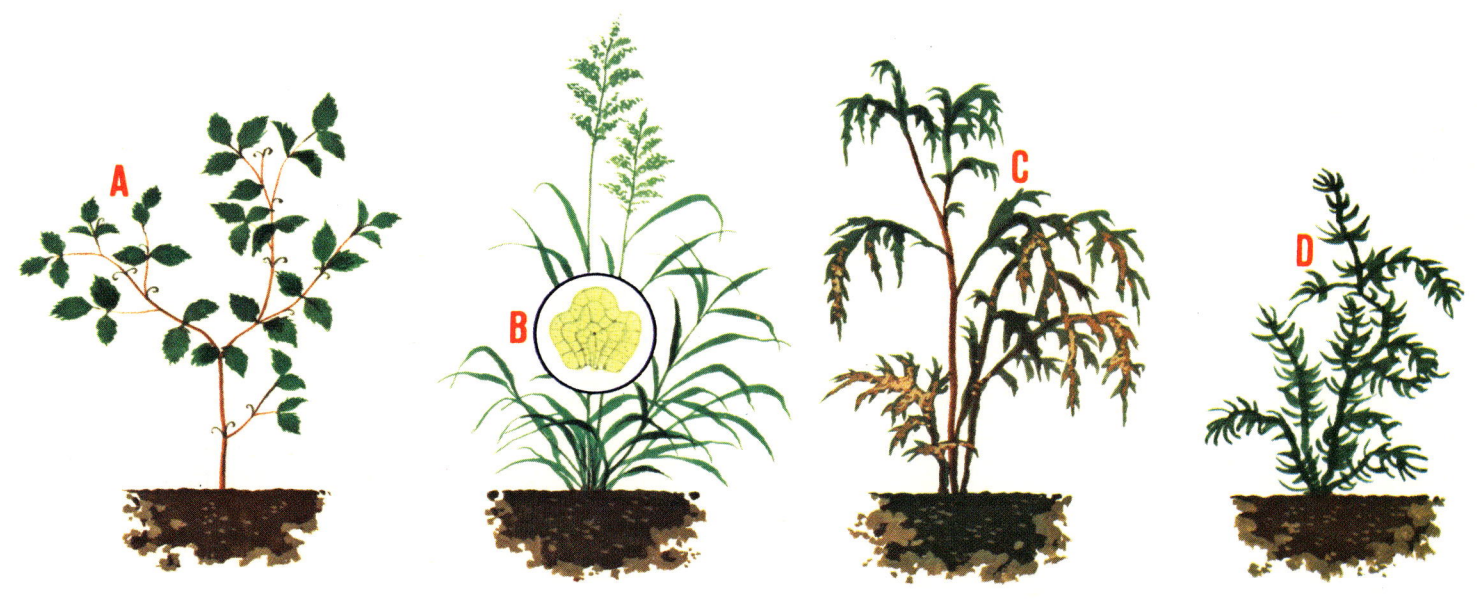

Left From the earliest times man has tried to cure himself of illness. Meadow saffron (top), ergot, obtained from fungus on rye (centre), and foxglove, which gives us the drug digitalis (bottom), have all been useful to the modern pharmaceutical industry. And although many totally new drugs have been invented in the laboratory many old remedies have been found to have a solid scientific basis. **Right** A modern pharmaceutical laboratory.

pharmaceutical industry. These include spurred rye (ergot), belladonna (deadly nightshade), foxglove (digitalis), meadow saffron, camomile, juniper, thorn apple, the caster oil plant, valerian, milkwort, thyme, rhubarb—but the list is endless.

Pharmaceutical chemistry is a vast field that we can only touch upon here. Among the anaesthetics we must mention that old stand-by chloroform, and the more modern diethyl ether, vinyl ether, trichloroethylene, cyclopropane and thiobarbiturates. Hypnotics and narcotics, such as the bromides, induce a sound sleep. Analgesics are pain-killers. These include morphine (and its derivative heroin), procaine, codeine and ethyl chloride. A common disinfectant is ethanol, but we must not forget isopropanol, which is remarkably effective, or iodine and hydrogen peroxide.

Many hormones have a vital use in curative medicine. Insulin, for the control of diabetes, and thyroid hormones are of great importance. Vitamins are also produced by the pharmaceutical industry. Vitamin C (ascorbic acid), unlike nearly all the other vitamins, is not extracted from organic substances, but is synthesized. We must also mention the famous antibiotic penicillins, and tetracycline, neomycin and carbomycin, all of them widely used in the unending fight against disease.

Toxicology is an important branch of pharmaceutical chemistry. It involves the study of toxic (poisonous) substances, the treatment of cases of poisoning, and research into drugs that can be prepared from naturally toxic substances. There are many different types of toxic substance, ranging from those found in various species of fungus and other vegetable matter, to animal poisons, for example the venom of such snakes as the viper and the adder, and that secreted by the scorpion.

We shall end by mentioning what might appear to be an extremely frivolous example of applied chemistry, but which in fact involves a great deal of painstaking research by highly-trained chemists—the cosmetics industry. Beauty-care products no longer just include preparations to enhance the appearance of the face, the hair, and to make people sweet-smelling. They now cater for the needs of the whole body, and therefore contain antiseptic ingredients, vitamins, decongestants and disinfectants.

6 The future

Above Chemicals do not always help us. For example, the venom produced by the puff adder and the toxin in the lethal mushroom, *Amanita phalloides*, are both deadly poisons.

Now that we have looked at the range of chemicals available to us today we can see that no industry could hope to survive without the advances made by chemists. Over the past 100 years huge strides have been made and every year there are new discoveries that enable us to make advances, improve our standard of living and manufacture helpful products. Who would have thought 100 years ago of the vast changes that chemists have brought to society?

A century ago we were totally dependent on coal as the major fuel and oil was in its infancy. Today on the one hand we have a more economic and thoughtful use of these fossil fuels and the new industry of nuclear power. On the other, the discoveries made about the elements over the past 100 years are helping us to harness the power of solar and wind energy.

On the way to today's relatively advanced society we have discovered the advantages—and disadvantages—of being able to replace the natural nitrogen in the soil so that our crops grow bigger and stronger. And we have been able to overcome some of the natural plagues such as insects that have dogged our footsteps since the earliest times. In the developed countries, modern drugs have cut down the number of deaths from disease and anaesthetics have cut down the pain and shock of surgery. But it is instructive to look at the side-effects of progress.

To be sure, we have a booming chemical industry which gives millions of people jobs both directly and indirectly. But that same industry produces the fumes that cause all manner of modern ailments and some spectacular accidents have taught us that there is often a price to be paid for progress.

Insects that carry diseases like malaria and sleeping sickness are now becoming resistant to the insecticides that were brand new and so very effective only a short time ago. And as we have eliminated the age old diseases so new ones have come to take their place—the so-called stress diseases of modern society that drugs alone cannot cure.

In all, we have to remember that in the last century we have made enormous strides in the knowledge of our world and the substances that make it what it is. That is the science of chemistry and we should never forget just how useful it has been in the past and will be in the future. But we also have to remember to treat the world responsibly and learn from the mistakes of the past when new discoveries are made. In the past the consequences of mistakes have not been too much for the natural systems to bear. It is to be hoped that future errors, if they are made on a large scale, will not prove to be irreversibly damaging.

Glossary
Periodic Table
Index

Glossary

acid A substance which liberates hydrogen ions in solution. The hydrogen may be replaced by a metal to form a salt. Acids usually have a sour taste and turn litmus indicator red.

alchemy A medieval art with only flimsy scientific foundations, the main object of which was to find a way of transmuting the so-called base metals, lead and iron, into gold using the imaginary philosophers' stone. Alchemists also hoped to find a magical substance called the elixir of life. Many of its roots are to be found in Arabic cultures and not all the work done over the centuries was rubbish. For example, the alchemist Geber described the preparation of sulphuric acid and silver nitrate more than 12 centuries ago. One of the most famous English alchemists was Roger Bacon (1214–1293) who also devoted himself to philosophy and astrology.

allotrope Some elements can exist in more than one form and these are called allotropes. Phosphorus, for example, can exist in a red or white form and tin has two common forms, grey and white. Allotropes often have different chemical properties too. White phosphorus burns spontaneously in air whereas the red form which we use in match heads does not.

alloy Alloys are formed by heating two or more metals at a high temperature so that they form a homogeneous mixture that has new properties different from those of the individual constituents. Sometimes non-metals may be added to get the desired properties; e.g. carbon is often added to steel to make it hard.

apatite A calcium mineral also containing fluorine and phosphorus which appears in several different forms and colours. It is found to make glass-like hexagonal crystals.

Aristotle (384–322 BC) A Greek philosopher who invented the theory that there are four elements in the universe: fire, air, earth and water. This concept was often quoted as a fact by alchemists.

atom The smallest portion of an element that can take part in a chemical reaction.

atomic theory A hypothesis about the structure of matter put forward by the British chemist Dalton in the mid nineteenth century. It assumes that matter is made up of small invisible particles called atoms and that the atoms of any one element are identical in all respects.

atomic weight The relative mass of an atom when compared with an atom of carbon. Thus hydrogen with an atomic weight of one is one-twelfth the mass of an atom of carbon which has an atomic weight of 12 and is taken as the standard.

base A substance that liberates hydroxyl groups (OH) in solution with water. They react with acids to form a salt plus water only.

Becquerel, Henri (1852–1908) A French scientist who was first to notice in 1896 that uranium gave off radiation which would leave a trace on a photographic plate.

Bessemer process A process used for purifying crude iron after it has been extracted from iron ore in the blast furnace. Impurities are removed by a blast of oxygen through the molten metal. The impurities form a scum which can be removed or are oxidized to gases.

Boyle, Robert (1627–91) British chemist who began the steady march towards modern chemistry by rejecting Aristotle's theory of the four elements and came near to the modern definition of the elements.

catalyst A substance that alters the velocity of a chemical reaction without being chemically changed itself. Catalysts are usually used to speed up reactions, but they can be used to slow reactions down too. A good example is iron powder which is used industrially to speed up the manufacture of ammonia from nitrogen and hydrogen.

caustic soda Sodium hydroxide which dissolves in water to form a strongly alkaline solution which turns litmus blue. It is one of the strongest of the bases and is used in the soap and dyestuffs industries.

cellulose The tough fibres found in all plant cells, it is used extensively in industry. Cotton wool and paper are made almost entirely of it. Cellulose is also much used for making yarns, fibres and explosives.

chalcedony A variety of impure silica (silicon dioxide). It is shiny and fibrous.

chlorophyll A green pigment found in all green plants. It enables them to convert carbon dioxide and water into sugars during photosynthesis (synthesis by light) by absorbing solar energy.

compound A substance consisting of two or more elements chemically united in definite proportions by weight.

Curie, Marie (1867–1934) French research chemist who first isolated the element radium from the uranium ore pitchblende. She also isolated the rare element polonium and in 1911 was awarded the Nobel Prize for chemistry.

dendrites Crystallized material in the form of tree or branch-like shapes in rock strata.

deuterium Heavy hydrogen: an isotope of hydrogen in which the nucleus of the atom is twice as heavy as that of ordinary hydrogen.

diodes Small devices used in radios for rectification of current and demodulation.

druses Irregular groupings of crystals on flat surfaces.

ductility The property of being able to be drawn out into fine wire. Most metals are extremely ductile, e.g. copper which is commonly used for electrical wiring.

electrolysis The chemical decomposition of certain substances by an electric current passed through the substance in a dissolved or molten state. Such substances are ionized into electrically-charged ions and when the electric current is passed through they travel to the oppositely-charged electrode, there to give up their charge and be deposited or liberated as gases. Thus copper can be plated onto metal, or water broken down into its component elements, hydrogen and oxygen.

electrolyte A compound which in solution conducts an electric current and is simultaneously decomposed by it.

electron A tiny negatively-charged particle present in all atoms. Its negative charge is opposite and equal to that of the proton. Hydrogen, the smallest of all the atoms, has one electron and one proton.

enzymes Complex organic compounds present in living organisms. They act as catalysts in digestion and fermentation.

Frasch process Used in the United States for extracting sulphur from underground deposits. The sulphur is melted by steam then pumped to the surface by water as a slurry. The sulphur obtained from these deposits, located mainly in the Southern states, is more than 99 per cent pure.

Galvani, Luigi (1737–98) Italian scientist who invented the zinc plating process for protecting steel from corrosion, called galvanization after him.

geodes Irregular groupings of crystals inside a cavity.

glycoside Complex compound consisting of a sugar, generally glucose, and other substances. Common in vegetable matter.

guano Accumulated waste matter from sea birds rich in nitrogen and phosphorus derived from the largely fish diet of the birds. A valuable fertilizer, it is mined in large quantities in Chile and Peru.

Haber, Fritz (1868–1934) German chemist who invented the Haber process for making ammonia by combining hydrogen (from coal gas) with nitrogen (from the air). The process came into full-scale use in Germany just before the start of World War I and gave the Germans a valuable lead over the Allies in explosives production and enabled them to defy the naval blockade on the import of ammonium products.

haemoglobin The substance that makes blood red. It is a complex protein consisting of four chains with an iron core and serves as the substance that transports oxygen from the lungs to the tissues.

hormones Substances produced by certain cells and glands in plants and animals. They pass from their points of secretion into the bloodstream which carries them to various organs to stimulate activity.

ion An electrically-charged atom or group of atoms. Positively-charged atoms (cations) have fewer electrons than necessary to be electrically neutral. Negatively-charged ions (anions) have more electrons than necessary for electrical neutrality.

ion exchange The substitution of one group of ions by another. A good example of this is in water softeners where calcium and magnesium ions which make water hard are exchanged for sodium and potassium ions which make water soft.

isomerism The existence of two or more chemical compounds with the same molecular formula but having different properties because of a different arrangement of atoms within the molecule. For example ammonium cyanate with the formula NH_4CNO and urea with the formula $CO(NH_2)_2$ are isomers. They have the same number of atoms in their molecules, but totally different chemical properties.

isotope A form of an element having a different atomic weight from the normal form due to a difference in the mass of the nucleus. This does not affect its chemical properties.

jasper A variety of chalcedony.

Lavoisier, Antoine-Laurent (1743–94) French chemist and physicist. He did important work on combustion and eventually disproved once and for all the phlogiston theory by showing that in combustion the elements combine with oxygen. He was guillotined during the French Revolution.

litmus Common chemical indicator used in the laboratory to show whether a substance is acidic or alkaline. Acids turn litmus red while alkalis turn it blue. A purple dye in its neutral state, it is extracted from lichens.

Mendeleev, Dmitri Ivanovitch (1834–1907) Russian chemist who devised the Periodic Table of the elements. His discovery has enabled scientists to predict accurately the properties and atomic weights of undiscovered elements. His own discoveries—predicted from his table—include scandium, germanium and rhenium.

mildew Grey-green fungus often found on plants in damp conditions. Sulphur dusting is often used to prevent it in vineyards.

molecule The smallest particle of an element or compound that can exist independently and show the characteristic chemical properties of that element or compound. Some elements, notably the metals, have only one atom in their molecules but others, for example nitrogen, have two atoms in the molecule.

neutron An elementary particle with a neutral charge found in all atomic nuclei except in normal hydrogen which has only one proton and one electron.

nucleic acids Organic substances of very high molecular weight essential to the life of animal and vegetable cells. Their purpose is to transmit the hereditary characteristics (DNA) or to manufacture proteins (RNA).

oxidation The combination of a substance with oxygen to form an oxide, or the increase in the proportion of oxygen atoms in a compound that already contains oxygen. The term is also used to describe a reduction in the proportion of hydrogen in a molecule or its total elimination.

peat Accumulation of vegetable sediments that are partially decomposed. Peat represents an intermediate stage in the formation of coal and is itself used as a fuel.

phlogiston theory A theory of combustion that held sway from the early Middle Ages until finally disproved by Lavoisier in the eighteenth century. Substances that burned in air were said to contain a magical constituent called phlogiston which burned away, leaving ash.

photochemical reactions Chemical reactions which are initiated, assisted or accelerated by exposure to light. For example hydrogen and chlorine react together explosively in sunlight but only slowly in the dark.

proton An elementary particle with an electrical charge equal to that of an electron but a mass nearly 2,000 times greater.

purple A natural dye taken from certain marine molluscs, it was much prized in the ancient world. Hence we have the phrase 'Royal Purple' because only Roman emperors were allowed to wear clothes of the rare and valuable colour. In the early nineteenth century the English chemist William Perkin discovered how to make purple artificially and founded an important industry on it.

reduction A reduction or elimination of oxygen in a molecule or the increase in the amount of hydrogen.

rose quartz Crystalline structures reminiscent of flower petals. They occur chiefly in gypsum.

stalactites Accumulations of calcium carbonate descending from the roofs of caves. They are slowly formed by the continuous evaporation of water saturated with calcium carbonate dripping from the roof of the cavern. *Stalagmites* grow upwards by a similar process.

sublimation Direct conversion of a substance from a solid to a gaseous state or vice versa without passing through a liquid stage. Iodine crystals undergo this type of transformation when heated.

transuranic elements Elements coming beyond uranium in the Periodic Table. They are all elements with atomic numbers above 92 and do not occur naturally. They can be obtained by means of nuclear reactions.

travertine Uncrystallized calcite that is porous and opaque.

tritium An isotope of hydrogen where the nucleus is three times the mass of normal hydrogen.

ultraviolet radiation Electromagnetic radiation of medium wavelength coming between visible light and X-rays. Solar radiation is a rich source and it is this radiation that gives us a suntan.

Wohler, Friedrich (1800–82) German chemist who in 1828 showed that the organic chemical urea could be synthesized from inorganic compounds. This dismissed the 'vital force' theory of organic chemicals and opened the way for the scientific study of organic chemicals.

THE PERIODIC TABLE

An arrangement of the chemical elements in order of their atomic numbers—the number of electrons rotating around the nucleus—in such a way as to show the similarities of elements in their family groups. In this way the properties of any element can be predicted. The Russian chemist Mendeleev first worked out the table.

IA	IIA	IIIA	IVA	VA	VIA	VIIA	VIII			IB	IIB	IIIB	IVB	VB	VIB	VIIB	O
Hydrogen H 1																Hydrogen H 1	Helium He 2
Lithium Li 3	Beryllium Be 4											Boron B 5	Carbon C 6	Nitrogen N 7	Oxygen O 8	Fluorine F 9	Neon Ne 10
Sodium Na 11	Magnesium Mg 12											Aluminium Al 13	Silicon Si 14	Phosphorus P 15	Sulphur S 16	Chlorine Cl 17	Argon Ar 18
Potassium K 19	Calcium Ca 20	Scandium Sc 21	Titanium Ti 22	Vanadium V 23	Chromium Cr 24	Manganese Mn 25	Iron Fe 26	Cobalt Co 27	Nickel Ni 28	Copper Cu 29	Zinc Zn 30	Gallium Ga 31	Germanium Ge 32	Arsenic As 33	Selenium Se 34	Bromine Br 35	Krypton Kr 36
Rubidium Rb 37	Strontium Sr 38	Yttrium Y 39	Zirconium Zr 40	Niobium Nb 41	Molybdenum Mo 42	Technetium Tc 43	Ruthenium Ru 44	Rhodium Rh 45	Palladium Pd 46	Silver Ag 47	Cadmium Cd 48	Indium In 49	Tin Sn 50	Antimony Sb 51	Tellurium Te 52	Iodine I 53	Xenon Xe 54
Caesium Cs 55	Barium Ba 56	Lanthanum La 57	Hafnium Hf 72	Tantalum Ta 73	Tungsten W 74	Rhenium Re 75	Osmium Os 76	Iridium Ir 77	Platinum Pt 78	Gold Au 79	Mercury Hg 80	Thallium Tl 81	Lead Pb 82	Bismuth Bi 83	Polonium Po 84	Astatine At 85	Radon Rn 86
Francium Fr 87	Radium Ra 88	Actium Ac 89															

Cerium Ce 58	Praseodymium Pr 59	Neodymium Nd 60	Promethium Pm 61	Samarium Sm 62	Europium Eu 63	Gadolinium Gd 64	Terbium Tb 65	Dysprosium Dy 66	Holmium Ho 67	Erbium Er 68	Thulium Tm 69	Ytterbium Yb 70	Lutetium Lu 71
Thorium Th 90	Protactinium Pa 91	Uranium U 92	Neptunium Np 93	Plutonium Pu 94	Americium Am 95	Curium Cm 96	Berkelium Bk 97	Californium Cf 98	Einsteinium Es 99	Fermium Fm 100	Mendelevium Md 101	Nobelium No 102	Lawrencium Lr 103

Index